Praise for *In the Teahouse of Experience*

"*Wah!* So wonderful to have these enlightening words under the name 'Sufi' to help humanity make its way from confusion to loving kindness and compassion. Thank you for this beautiful book crafted with so much care; may it bring joy and guidance to every one who has the good fortune of opening her pages!"

— Pir Shabda Kahn, head of the Sufi Ruhaniat Order, co-author of *Physicians of the Heart*

"What a balm for the soul. I began reading Pir Netanel's book and my heart and spirit were deeply fed. He shares the deep principles of Sufism with a grace and simplicity that is accessible and relatable. I could feel the deep parallels to the Toltec and Buddhist practices that nourish me, finding myself alternately crying and laughing as I felt these connections. I highly recommend this book."

— Brenda Salgado, founder of Nepantla Consulting, and author of *Real World Mindfulness for Beginners*

"Add this treasure to your spiritual library of authentic Sufi texts, and read it again and again for the stories, for the wisdom, and then just for the joy of being with one of God's friends."

— Pir Puran Bair, co-founder of the Institute for Applied Meditation on the Heart, co-author of *Living from the Heart*

"Join centuries of Sufis—'Drink with the Beloved'—this steaming tasty tea. Bright with understanding, *In the Teahouse of Experience* is a beautifully written glimpse into leaves of mysticism, moistened and fragrant."

— Tamam Kahn, author of *Untold, A History of the Wives of Prophet Muhammad* and *Fatima's Touch*

"Open these pages and drink deeply from the insight and wisdom of a gifted teacher, storyteller, and poet. Thank you Pir Netanel for sharing so generously from the spiritual traditions that have nourished you!"

—Rabbi Or N. Rose, director of the Miller Center for Interreligious Learning & Leadership, and co-author of *God in All Moments*

"From the first story I was hooked; Netanel Miles-Yépez has managed—through the power of his storytelling and a close attention to his own spiritual life—to meet the need of our minds to understand, the longing of our hearts to feel the closeness of the Beloved, and to shine a light in our souls. By journeying through the essential elements of the Sufi path we discover how to walk in the mystery of life with authenticity, passion, and care. The only other thing you can add to make it a richer experience is a nice cup of tea!"

— Deepa Gulrukh Patel, Sufi teacher, group facilitator, and international coordinator of the Sufi Zenith Camp

"*In the Teahouse of Experience* is a wonderful guide for the Sufi seeker; truly one of the best books on Universalist Sufism available today!"

— Rev. Adam Bucko, co-author of *Occupy Spirituality* and *The New Monasticism*

In the Teahouse of Experience

Nine Talks on the Path of Sufism

Pir Netanel Miles-Yépez

The Inayati-Maimuni Order
Boulder, Colorado
2020

*"The old shall be renewed,
and the new shall be made holy."*
— Rabbi Avraham Yitzhak Kook

This book has been produced for the Inayati-Maimuni Order in cooperation with Albion-Andalus Books.

Albion-Andalus, Inc.
P. O. Box 19852
Boulder, CO 80308
www.albionandalus.com

Design and composition by Albion-Andalus Books
Cover design by D.A.M. Cool Graphics
Cover detail from the Peck *Shahnamah.* 16th century, Shiraz.
All illustrations by Netanel Miles-Yépez.
The illustration of "Zikr Calligraphy" (p.29) was designed by Sasha Gaynor.

ISBN-13: 978-1-953220-11-0 (Hardcover)
ISBN-13: 978-1-7348750-9-6 (Paperback)

Manufactured in the United States of America

For

Murshid Atum O'Kane

& Pir Puran Bair

Contents

Preface

The nine chapters of this book have their origin in eight talks and an interview given between 2015 to 2020. Many of the talks were given numerous times to different audiences around the country, being refined as the years passed. The versions contained herein have been edited for publication (adding a little material here and there, as well as some sources), but generally retain the structure, and hopefully, some of the colloquial flavor of the original talks. Although much of the content deals with Sufism in general, there is an emphasis on Chishti-Inayati Sufism as taught by Hazrat Inayat Khan, the lineage to which I belong. The quotes I use in the text are largely presented in the adapted forms in which I gave them in my oral talks, often being made gender inclusive for purposes of inclusion and accessibility.

The title, *In the Teahouse of Experience,* is drawn from the parable of tea told in the first chapter. For many years, I have used this parable as a means of introducing people to Sufism. Reading the parable, the meaning of the title will become apparent. The style of the title, however, I owe to the Nimatullahi master, Dr. Javad Nurbakhsh (1926-2008). His short works, *In the Tavern of Ruin* (1978) and *In the Paradise of the Sufis* (1979) influenced me greatly in the period shortly after my initiation, being broken down into convenient subjects with clear descriptions of different aspects of Sufi life and practice.

Having edited these talks into readable essays, I have had cause to reflect with gratitude on the teaching of my beloved *murshid,* Zalman Sulayman Schachter-Shalomi (1924-2014), and especially the two mentors he assigned to me: Murshid

Thomas Atum O'Kane and Pir Puran Bair. Having been asked to seek each of them out for specific guidance, I did so with an enthusiasm that each man met with kindness, generosity, and good grace. While the guidance they offered may have seemed small to them, the impact on me was profound, as I did my best to capitalize on every word of advice, devotedly practicing what I was given, and studying the writings of each with great avidity. To them I dedicate this book, hoping they may feel some sense of satisfaction for their investment in me.

I also wish to express my deep gratitude to my brother on the path, Pir Zia Inayat-Khan, with whom I worked so closely and fruitfully from 2015 to 2017, editing works on the *silsila* and the Inayati prayers, teaching together on various occasions, and taking many lovely walks. I am likewise indebted to Pir Shabda Kahn, who has been a good friend and mentor in recent years, and a fun dialogue partner. I have also had the privilege of working with numerous talented Inayati teachers over the last five years to whom I am indebted for their wisdom and friendly counsel, including: Murshida Tasnim Fernandez, Murshid Suhrawardi Gebel, Murshida Amina Hall, Murshida Taj Inayat, Murshid Himayat Inayati, Murshida Tamam Kahn, Murshid Gayan Macher, Murshid Wali Ali Meyer, Murshida Kainat Felicia Norton, Murshid Allaudin Ottinger, Murshida Aziza Scott, and Murshida Devi Tide.

I am likewise profoundly grateful to my treasured friend and companion, Jennifer Alia Wittman, who first invited me to teach at the Season of the Rose, the annual summer school of the Inayati Order at the Abode of the Message in New Lebanon, New York, June 26th to July 1st, 2015, for which the "Sufism and the Inner Life" interview was prepared, and again at Lewis and Clark College in Portland, Oregon, July 6th-11th, 2016, where four of these talks ("The Story of Tea," "Circling the Temple of God," "The Three Deaths of Love," and "Meditation of the Heart") were delivered; in many ways, you were my partner in all of this work, and its great inspiration.

To my friend, Al Bellenchia, who invited me to become teacher-in-residence and later spiritual director of the Abode of the Message in New Lebanon, New York, from August of 2016 to August of 2017, where I gave my "Eight Aspects of Sufi Mindfulness" talk, and refined several others, thank you.

Thanks to my dear friend and dialogue partner, Deepa Gulrukh Patel, with whom I taught "Rasa Shastra: Exploring Love, Intimacy, Sex, and Relationships in Sufism," May 12th-14th, 2017, during which another version of "The Three Deaths of Love" was given. Thanks also to my friends, Brett and Abigail Larson (Bob and Lana Kosik, too) who hosted my partner and I during the Season of the Rose in Portland, Oregon in 2016, and for other talks in the years since; and to Lucas Kestrel Sego who so ably assisted me during the Season of the Rose talks in Portland, Oregon.

Other friends, colleagues in different spheres, and students in my meditation trainings who deserve thanks for their help during this period include: Diane Atayna Austen, Tony M. Latif Bedell, Jessica Bromby, Andy Bruce, Andrea Saraswati Burke, Debra-Sue Cope, Blair Mahboob Davis, Chuck Jameel Davis, Mariana Nabila Evans, Darakshan Farber, Aimee Johnson, Rebecca Juan, Mirza Inayat Khan, Satya Inayat Khan, Sukhawat Ali Khan, Saiqa Latif, Sarah Leila Manolson, Amanda Salima McCall, Khaldun Mendel, Gene Hallaj Michalenko, Chris Akbar Miller, Linda Nasreen Moayedi, Ryan Rehan Morey, Anne Roshan Peay, Ibrahim Pedriñan, Robert Premack, Sara Rain, Nasiban Schatz, Samuel Vilayat Schatz, Peter Halim Schein, Gabriel Steadman, Evan Thaler-Null, Wendy Jehanara Tremayne, Wendy Waduda Welsh, Murshida Eileen Alia Yager, Evan Young, and Janice Wahida Young.

I am likewise grateful to Naropa University and its Department of Wisdom Traditions for providing such a hospitable home for my yearly "Sufi Retreat Intensives," where almost all of these talks were originally given or later refined. Specifically, I would like to thank: President Charles Lief, a wise, supportive, compassionate, and conscientious leader; our diligent department head, Dr. Phil Stanley; and my friends and colleagues, Lisa Chatham, Dr. Amelia Hall, Dr. Zvi Ish-Shalom, Yogi Nataraja Kallio, Crista Lawson, Dr. Judith Simmer-Brown, Rachel Solum, Dr. Ben Williams, and Dr. Stephanie Yuhas.

I am especially indebted to my beautiful and heartful murids who have listened to these talks many times, helping out with the book in various tasks related to it, especially Daniel Jami' who thoughtfully and diligently proofread the book, Sasha Salika Gaynor who helped with the glossary and designed one of the illustrations, Yasha Sana'i Wagner, Erica Shamah Leitz, Jenna Nabilah Jennings, Joel Amin Berndt, Ayah Lehtonen, Connor Khalil Marvin, Tim Shams Holbert, Sahar Suaid, Heidi Safiyya Lukinac, and Gregory Taha Yamada. Thanks also to Joseph Elsberry, Sarah McKay, Awa Faridah Ndiaye, Michael Ranieri, Elvira Sevilla-Moran, Helene Van den Berg, Bridget Winningham, and Declan, too, who were generous with their time. And to Eve Ilsen who has been the most gracious host for so many evenings of *zikr* and *soḥbet* in Pir Zalman's *zawiyya*.

And finally, during this long period of confinement amid much fear and concern the world over, in which I have written the majority of this book, to my loving and supportive partner, Jamelah Nabil Zidan, you have been a godsend and a healing balm; thank you.

Netanel Mu'in ad-Din Miles-Yépez
Boulder, Colorado, March 29th, 2020

"According to our evolution, we know truth."

— *The Bowl of Saqi*

tasawwuf

The Story of Sufism

The Foundations of Traditional and Universalist Sufism *

Once, long ago, tea was unknown outside of China. But slowly, word of this 'celestial' or 'heavenly drink' made its way down the Silk Road and into the various kingdoms it connected.

In one of these kingdoms, a kingdom called Inja—*'here'*—the king had heard rumors of the celestial drink, and being curious to know if such a thing actually existed, decided to send ambassadors to the Emperor of China, seeking permission to taste this thing called 'tea' for themselves.

Thus, the ambassadors of Inja made the long journey up the Silk Road into China where, finally reaching the gates of the Emperor's palace, they were admitted and granted an audience with the Emperor himself.

"Your Radiant Highness, Son of Heaven," they said ceremonially, standing before the emperor, "we have been sent by the King of Inja to request the honor of tasting the celestial drink known as 'tea.'"

The Emperor of China was silent. He would not deign to speak to the lowly ambassadors of the insignificant kingdom of Inja, but merely gestured to his ministers, who showed the ambassadors into another chamber set with tables, where they were served the celestial drink, tea.

* An edited version of a talk originally given in Portland, Oregon on July 7th, 2016 at Lewis and Clark College for the Season of the Rose, the annual summer school of the Inayati Order.

Sitting at the low tables, tasting the tea for themselves, the ambassadors said to one another—"It's wonderful! Both stimulating and relaxing at the same time! It truly is the celestial drink!"

Pleased with themselves and their success, the ambassadors of Inja began the long journey back home. Only now, they decided to take their time and see a little of China, stopping various places to see the sights and staying in different roadhouses to sample the local cuisine. But in so doing, they soon discovered something profoundly disturbing to them . . . *Everyone was drinking tea, both peasants and royalty alike!*

On returning to Inja and the court of the king, the latter asked them, "Were you successful in your mission?"

"Yes," said the ambassadors, tentatively, "but . . ."

"But what?" said the king.

"Well, we *did* make it to the palace of the Emperor of China, and we *were* served something wonderful that was *called,* 'tea' . . . but we suspect that they may have played a joke on us, or decided not to serve us the real tea. For we later discovered that this same drink was offered all over China, and served to both peasants and royalty alike!"

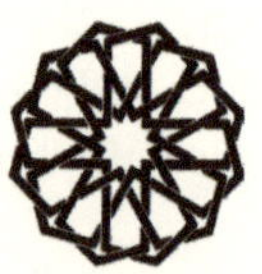

In another country along the Silk Road known as Anja—*'there'*—was a great philosopher, indeed, the greatest philosopher of the region, whose primary interest was tea. He thought constantly of tea, speculating about it and collecting information from travelers in his notebooks. Some said it was a dry leaf; some said a liquid. Some said it was a drink, greenish in color; some said golden. Some said it was sweet; while others said bitter. In time, this philosopher compiled the world's greatest collection of information about tea, and had written the authoritative treatise on the subject, becoming the most renowned authority in the whole region . . . *but he had never tasted it!*

Elsewhere, in a land called Mazhab—*'sectarianism'*—they had actually managed to procure a single bag of tea! And one day each year, they would attach this little sachet containing dried tea leaves by four thin strings to two great staves, which four large and grim-faced men rested on their shoulders, carrying it with ritual solemnity through the streets of the capital. On that day, all the city's inhabitants would leave work and come out of their homes to witness the holy procession. And when the sacred bag of tea passed before them, all would bow down and prostrate in fear and trembling.

And this is the way it was for a long time, until one year, on the day of the holy procession, a visitor to the capital remained standing while all the city's inhabitants prostrated before the sacred bag of tea. Laughing out loud, he said, "*No-o-o-o,* you idiots! You have to pour boiling water on it!"

An audible gasp went through the crowd. The grim-faced priests carrying the tea bag turned to look at the man in both horror and anger. Then, with a look and an angry gesture, they ordered the religious police to arrest the heretic, this enemy of religion, for suggesting the destruction of the holy tea! The police immediately seized the man and he was later executed in the most horrible ways.

Fortunately for us, before this sad incident, the man had confided the secret of tea to a few friends in the city, and had bequeathed to them the tea he had brought with him on his journey. But having seen what happened to their friend, they now knew not to make the same mistake of talking about infusing the tea with boiling water, or of drinking it openly. Instead, they gathered in secret to do so, and if anyone happened to ask them what it was they were drinking, they would answer simply, "Just a little medicine."

In this way, they grew in wisdom, until one day, the wisest among them said this . . . "The one who tastes, *knows;* the one who tastes not, *knows not.* Stop talking about the 'celestial drink,' but serve it at your banquets. Those who like it will ask for more; those who do not are not fitted to be tea-drinkers. Close the shop of argument and open the tea-house of experience."

Thus, this circle of secret tea-drinkers became the first merchants of tea. Being already merchants of fabrics and jewels, traveling tradesmen of all sorts, they took their tea with them wherever they traveled along the Silk Road. And wherever they might stop, they would take out a little tea and brew it, offering to share it with whoever might be near. This was the beginning of the chaikhanas, the tea-houses that then popped-up all over Central Asia, spreading the true use and reputation of tea far and wide.[1]

Traditional Definitions of Sufism

For over a thousand years, Sufis have routinely learned and recited various definitions of Sufism as a kind of spiritual practice, as a way of continually 'course-correcting' and guiding themselves back to the ideals of Sufism. Thus, they have often asked themselves the question, 'What is Sufism?' The Parable of Tea is one answer. Thus, we might look more closely at it and consider what it is trying to say.

First, we have the curious king of 'here'—Inja—who wants to know if there really is such a thing as 'tea,' which might stand for Sufism or mystical experience. But, being a rather ordinary or unremarkable sort of king, he does not go out in search of it himself, but sends ambassadors or emissaries in his stead. The emissaries actually taste the tea for themselves, but are convinced that it cannot be the 'real thing,' because people of all classes and stations drink it. In other words, they are elitists who cannot accept that mystical experience is something available to everyone.

Then we have the great philosopher of 'there'—Anja—who is the world's greatest authority on 'tea,' though he has never tasted it. Thus, his is only head-knowledge, as opposed to the more substantive experiential knowledge. He is like the academic scholars of Sufism who can describe all of its characteristics based on the reports and writings of others, but who have never tasted the heart-broken love and self-obliterating passion it offers.

Elsewhere, in the land of 'sectarianism'—Mazhab—they actually worship the 'tea,' but in a dry form. This is religion without spirituality, without the infusion of spirit, the one thing necessary to bring it to life, allowing people to benefit from it. The priests of religion celebrate and defend the 'dry form,' or potential of religion, often forgetting that the purpose of religion is not merely to preserve the religion itself, but to aid one in transformation. In so doing, they become worshippers of religion instead of God. Thus, Sufis have been known to say . . .

"A Sufi's religion is God."[2]

Obviously, this is a Sufi critique of religion, a way of suggesting to the orthodox—'You have become worshippers of Islam,' or 'Christianity' or 'Judaism,' as the case may be, 'and have forgotten *God* in your observance of religion. Whereas, God *is* our religion!' That is to say, the direct experience of God is a Sufi's religion. Indeed, it was in the context of such a critique—in rebellion against conventional religion—that historical Sufism was born.

Sufis often say that 'Sufism has always existed,' being the deep impulse of the heart that seeks wholeness in divinity or the sacred, which is found in every religious tradition. Thus, Muzaffer Ozak, the famous 20th-century Halveti-Jerrahi *shaykh,* says—"A river passes through many countries and each claims it for its own. But there is only one river."[3] In every land, that river is called by a different name in a different language, but there is only one river, flowing into one ocean.

Nevertheless, there is also a clear historical phenomenon with specific characteristics, called 'Sufism,' that has a definite context and origin in the Middle East. Personally, I like to explain this context through a parallel exploration of the possible etymological origins of the word, 'Sufi.'[4]

Among the most commonly suggested origins is the Arabic word, *suffah,* 'bench,' which is itself a reference to the *ahl as-suffah,* 'people of the bench,' or *ashab as-suffah,* 'companions of the bench.'[5] In the time of the prophet Muḥammad, *alayhi as-salam,* 'peace be upon him,' the 'people of the bench' were an apparently impoverished group of companions of the Prophet who never seemed to leave the bench outside the *masjid,* or mosque, in Medina.[6] They were probably looked upon by many as lazy and indolent; but it is said that they were actually so God-intoxicated that all they wanted to do was remain in prayer close to the mosque. They could never do enough practice, never talk enough about God, so they never left the precincts of the mosque! Thus, these "people of the bench," according to some, are considered the first Sufis.

However, another legend says that Sufis, at first, were actually a nameless, wandering band of mystics, who roamed the world in search of the *qutb,* the 'axis' or 'pole' of spirituality in any given age. Thus, in the time of the prophet Muḥammad, they were magnetically drawn to Medina, the city of the Prophet, where they recognized him as the *qutb* and embraced Islam. Thus, the originally nameless form of Sufism took on an Arabic character and name, and became associated with Islam, though it never lost its essentially universalist spiritual outlook. Some even say that this group of wandering seekers, arriving in Medina without any other material aim or intention, became the 'people of the bench.'[7]

Later, this recognition of the nameless origins of Sufism led one great Sufi master to admonish his fellow Sufis with this famous statement . . .

"Once, Sufism was a reality without a name;
now it is but a name without a reality."[8]

Another explanation of the origin of the word 'Sufi' is the Arabic *safa,* 'pure,' from which we get, *tasawwuf.*[9] In English, we speak of the tradition of 'Sufism,' but that is merely an Anglicized form of the Arabic word, *tasawwuf,* meaning 'purification,' a process or path of continual purification, purifying oneself from the more spiritually deadening effects of the ego.

Nevertheless, historically and linguistically, scholars tend to agree that the most likely origin of the word, 'Sufi,' is the Arabic word *suf,* 'wool,' a reference to the simple woolen cloaks worn by early Muslim ascetics in the 8th and 9th-century in the Middle East.[10]

These pious Muslims were generally called *nussak* (sing. *nasik)* or 'ascetics,' and wore rough woolen garments, rejecting the decadent luxuries of the increasingly wealthy Islamic empire which, as they saw it, had lost its way. Their lifestyle was a protest and rebellion against the lax morality of the time. In just two hundred years, the originally poor and pious Muslim community of high ideals had become rich, bloated with wealth acquired through conquest, and extremely decadent. Thus, these early ascetic Muslims were trying to reestablish the ideals of Islam. To this end, they drew inspiration from the Christian Desert Fathers and Mothers (Abbas and Ammas) who lived in desert caves across the Middle East, and who were often known for wearing coarse woolen garments, an ascetic practice in that hot, dry climate.[11]

Indeed, stories of this cross-fertilization are preserved in the Sufi tradition, especially in an episode from the life of the great Sufi master, Ibrahim ibn Adham (d. 779), a king who gave up his kingdom to pursue God, who tells of a deep transmission of inner wisdom *(ma'rifah)* he received from a Christian ascetic.

According to the story, Ibrahim Adham once visited a Christian ascetic called Father Simeon in his desert cave in the mountains. He asked him, "How long have you been here, father?"

"Seventy years," Father Simeon answered.

"What food do you eat?" asked Ibrahim Adham.

"Why do you ask, my son?"

"I just want to know."

Father Simeon answered, "One chick pea a day."

Amazed, Ibrahim Adham said, "What moves your heart so much that you can live off so little?"

"Well, I'll tell you. Once a year," Father Simeon answered, "the people of the village below come up to celebrate my work here, adorning my cave and honoring me. Whenever I weary of this life, I think of that, and I can go on.

"Now, I ask *you*, what work of an hour would you endure for the whole glory of eternity?"

"Hearing this," Ibrahim Adham tells us, *"ma'rifah"*—the inner wisdom or experiential knowledge—"descended on me."[12]

For me, this is an amazing story, connecting the three great esoteric Abrahamic lineages. Just as the Desert Fathers and Mothers of Christianity were already the heirs of the Essenes, a Jewish mystical ascetic sect along the Dead Sea and the probable authors of the Dead Sea Scrolls, so too were the Sufis the heirs of the Desert Fathers and Mothers.[13]

These early Muslim ascetics, *nussak*, were even known to say that they followed the way of the Prophet Isa, or Jesus, who wore wool instead of the more comfortable cotton. In saying this, they were not proclaiming themselves converts to Christianity—they were still good Muslims—but recognizing that Jesus was a prophet in Islam whose model was closely aligned with their values. After all, they were rebelling against a corrupt government, and protesting the fact that Islam had become mixed-up with politics.[14] The prophet Muḥammad, of course, was considered the best possible ruler, a true philosopher- or prophet-king, but things had quickly degenerated after his passing. Aware of the problems of this model, these early proto-Sufis saw Jesus as a prophet who was not involved in politics or governance, leading an exemplary spiritual life. Thus, it likewise became a longstanding value among many Sufis not to become too deeply involved with powerbrokers or politics, nor to seek the influence of the powerful elite, whether those with great wealth or great political power.[15]

Within the larger ascetic protest movement of the 8th-century—roughly 200 years after the birth of Islam—were a fringe group called the *sufiyya,* the 'wool wearers,' which was likely a pejorative term originally used by their detractors to make fun of them. Nevertheless, the name stuck, and was eventually claimed by this group of spiritual idealists.[16] Indeed, one early master, accepting the more realistic derivation from *suf*, 'wool,' and combining it with the ideal of *safa*, 'purity,' famously said . . .

"The Sufi is the one who wears wool on top of purity."[17]

Likewise following the model of Jesus, these early Sufis emphasized Jesus' teachings on love, though, they did not need Christianity to show them the path to love of God. It was also there before them in the Qur'an *al-Karim* (5:54) . . .

"God loves them, and they love God."

Thus, some Sufis even came to say . . .

"Sufism is the religion of Love."[18]

It was not long before the early ascetic tradition of Sufism was transformed into a tradition oriented to the ideal and experience of divine love. This is perhaps owing to the influence of one individual more than any other, a woman and a former slave named Rabi'a al-Adawiyya or Rabi'a al-Basri (ca. 717-801).

Orphaned at an early age, Rabi'a was sold into slavery, but her owner, seeing that she spoke with God, became afraid and freed her.[19] After that, she began to wander, never leaving her devotions. She is said to have been a beautiful woman, but never married, devoting herself entirely to God. She is known to have said . . .

"I love You with two loves—
one that that is unworthy of You,
and one that is lost in You."[20]

And on another occasion . . .

"If I worship You for fear of hell, then send me there.
If I worship you out of a desire for heaven, then bar the gates.
But if I worship You for Your own sake,
then do not deny me the vision of Your eternal beauty."[21]

The most enduring image of Rabi'a al-Adawiyya for me is the description of her walking through the streets of Basra carrying a fiery torch in one hand and a bucket of water in the other. Some Sufis who saw her asked, "Lady Rabi'a, what are you going to do with these?"

She answered, "I'm going to set fire to paradise *(janna)* and douse the flames of hell *(jahannam),* so that both will cease to inspire desire and fear, that these veils may fall from their eyes, and the lover's purpose may become clear."[22]

Through her influence on many others, Sufism came to be oriented toward pure love and ecstatic experiences of union with the divine. Soon, practices developed around the remembrance of the divine beloved, such as *zikr* or *zikr Allah,* the mantric remembrance or recitation of the name of God. Sufism also developed practices of courting ecstasy with music and dance and the recitation of love poetry. Such sessions which put one in a state of ecstasy *(wajd)* were called *sama'* or 'hearing.' In these ecstatic states, it was said that the self *(nafs)* was annihilated *(fana')* in the experience of union with God.

Among the most famous of the early ecstatic Sufi masters was Mansur al-Hallaj (ca. 858-922), who is known for crying-out publicly in a moment of ecstasy, *An al-Haqq!*, "I am the Truth!"[23] . . . and then being executed as a heretic for it.[24] Of course, to the literal-minded, he seemed to be saying that *he* was God, that his individual ego had subsumed God, when actually he was saying quite the opposite, that his individual ego had been obliterated by God!

Does his story sound familiar? Clearly, al-Hallaj is the man from our story, the one visiting the land of sectarianism who laughs and cries out, "No, you idiots! You have to pour boiling water on it!"

Thus, the tea of the parable represents Sufism as a path emphasizing experience, specifically, the experience of 'tasting God,' or the sacred.

But the Parable of Tea is also a cautionary tale, describing a shift in the history of Sufism. Having seen what happened to al-Hallaj, and the general backlash against Sufism, many Sufis decided to go underground, practicing *zikr* or 'drinking their tea' in secret.[25] Thus, the admonition . . .

> The one who tastes, *knows;* the one who tastes not, *knows not.* Stop talking about the 'celestial drink,' but serve it at your banquets. Those who like it will ask for more; those who do not are not fitted to be tea-drinkers. Close the shop of argument and open the tea-house of experience.

This reminds me of Murshid Samuel Lewis' wonderful paraphrase of Abu Hamid Ghazzali's suggestion . . .

"Sufism is a school of experience, not dogmas."[26]

Sufism is not interested in trying to convince others to believe through argument, and does not have a specific set of beliefs to prescribe. It has specific teachings, of course, and a definite perspective oriented to divine love, but no dogmas about what you *must* believe. The idea of Sufism is to seek experience, your own experience. Beliefs should not be merely 'imported,' but formed from personal experience. In Sufism, you discover your own God or "God-ideal," as Hazrat Inayat Khan puts it.[27] The tradition is merely suggesting, 'Take these things in and try them out for yourself; discover your own relationship to the sacred.' The Sufi way is to share, not to impose, as the story illustrates . . .

> Thus, this circle of secret tea-drinkers became the first merchants of tea. Being already merchants of fabrics and jewels, traveling tradesmen of all sorts, they took their tea with them wherever they traveled along the Silk Road. And wherever they might stop, they would take out a little tea and brew it, offering to share it with whoever might be near. This was the beginning of the chaikhanas, the tea-houses that then popped-up all over Central Asia, spreading the true use and reputation of tea far and wide.

The chaikhanas or tea-houses, of course, refer to the many Sufi *turuq* or 'orders' (and their khanegahs) that soon arose, including the four great orders, the Chishti, Naqshbandi, Suhrawardi, and Qadiri.

The Emergence of Universalist Sufism

The Chishti lineage, which originally formed in Central Asia, eventually made its way into India with the great Sufi master, Khwaja Mu'in ad-Din Chishti (1141-1236), where it developed into a unique lineage incorporating Yogic practices and a specific musical lineage called, *qawwali.*

In 1910, a master in this lineage, Hazrat Inayat Khan (1882-1927), a great classical Indian musician in whom was also united the four great Sufi lineages, was charged by his master to bring Sufism into the West. In his master's words . . .

> Fare forth into the world, my child, and harmonize the East and the West with the harmony of your music. Spread the wisdom of Sufism abroad, for to this end art thou gifted by Allah, the most merciful and compassionate.[28]

Coming to the West, ostensibly as a musician, Inayat Khan gave concerts which were sometimes followed by lectures on Sufism. In San Francisco, in 1911, he met his first Western student, a child of Russian Jewish immigrants, named Ada Ginsberg Martin (1871-1947), who became the first American Sufi *murid* (initiate), and also the first American *murshida,* or acknowledged spiritual teacher of Sufism.[29]

But in taking on Western murids, it soon became clear to Inayat Khan that it was not necessarily his mission to spread Islam along with Sufism in the West. The people he was teaching were already Jews and Christians, whose religion was protected under the law of Islam. Thus, he began to introduce them to Sufism without Islam, as an esoteric path and set of teachings that might catalyze or 'turn on' what was dormant in their existing religious practice. In other words, he would teach them to "pour boiling water on it," to infuse it with Sufi spirituality.

Thus was born universalist Sufism, and also the Inayati lineage (as a new emphasis in a lineage is often marked by the addition of a name to it, often the name of the innovator). In time, Inayat Khan would propose yet another definition of Sufism, saying . . .

> *"If anybody asks you, 'What is Sufism?' . . . you may answer:*
> *'Sufism is the religion of the heart,*
> *the religion in which the most important thing*
> *is to seek God in the heart of humanity.'"*[30]

Now, some have asked, 'Is this still Sufism?' To this, I believe we can answer a clear, 'Yes.' Inayati or universalist Sufism maintains the traditional Sufi orientation to love and the heart, the commitment to personal spiritual experience through practice—through *zikr* (remembrance) and *muraqaba* (meditation)—and continues the great 1,400 year-old unbroken lineage, passed from Sufi master to Sufi master. Moreover,

Inayati Sufism is still completely in-line with and following the almost 800 year-old mandate of Khwaja Mu'in ad-Din Chishti to all Chishti Sufis . . .

Love all, and hate none.
Mere talk of peace will get you nothing.
Mere talk of God and religion will not take you far.

Bring out all of the latent powers of your being,
And reveal the full magnificence
Of your immortal self.[31]

Be charged with peace and joy,
And scatter them wherever you are,
And wherever you go.

Be a blazing fire of truth,
A beautiful blossom of love,
And a soothing balm of peace.

With your spiritual light,
Dispel the darkness of ignorance;
Dissolve the clouds of discord and war,
And spread goodwill, peace, and harmony among the people.

Never seek any help, charity, or favors
From anybody except God.

Never go to the courts of kings,
Nor refuse to bless and help the needy and the poor,
The widow or the orphan, if they come to your door.

This is your mission, to serve the people. . . .
Carry it out dutifully and courageously,
So that I, as your Pir-o-Murshid,

May not be ashamed of
Any shortcomings on your part
Before the Almighty God
And our holy predecessors
In the Sufi silsila
On the Day of Judgment.[32]

Zikr

Circling the Temple of God

The Remembrance of the Chishti-Inayati Sufis *

In Sufism, we sit together in a circle to emphasize our unity. The Sufi circle is called a *halqah,* or 'ring,' the symbol of our commitment to one another. In this 'ring,' we are bound as in a marriage to the sharing of an experience. Thus, a small group or community of Sufis is also called a *halqah* or 'Sufi circle,' because of what is shared between them.

The *halqah* formed for spiritual practice describes the boundaries of a ritual space. For this reason, we form and enter it intentionally, with an invocation. The invocation of the Inayati-Maimuni Sufis, based on that of Hazrat Inayat Khan, is done with both hands folded over the heart, lifting the head to the sky and allowing it to descend with the words, "This is not my body." Then, turning the head to the left shoulder, we allow it to loll and drift across the chest to the right shoulder, while saying, "This is the temple of the heart."[1] We then recite the primary prayer of the Inayati Sufis . . .

Toward the One,
The Perfection of Love, Harmony, and Beauty,
The Only Being,

* An edited version of a talk given in Portland, Oregon on July 8th, 2016 at Lewis and Clark College for the Season of the Rose, the annual summer school of the Inayati Order, and earlier talks in Boulder, Colorado, at Naropa University in the Fall of 2014.

United with all the Illuminated Souls
Who form the embodiment of the Master,
The Spirit of Guidance.

In this way, we create and enter a ritual space and atmosphere. The primary ritual or spiritual practice done in this atmosphere is called *zikr*.[2] The word *'zikr'* is most properly pronounced, *zik-rr* (hitting the *k* and adding a slight *rr* at the end); but this is difficult for English speakers, and thus it is commonly pronounced *zik-er* by English speaking Sufis. *Zikr* literally means, 'remembrance,' and takes its inspiration from the verse in the Qur'an (2:152) . . .

"Remember me that I may remember you."

Zikr is thus a practice of remembering God, the holy ground of our being, through repetition of a divine name or sacred formula.[3]

This might be as simple as reciting the name, *Allah*, or one of the other 'beautiful names' of God, such as *Ya Rahman* or *Ya Rahim*, or even a phrase such as *'Ishq Allah, ma'bud Allah*, 'God love, God beloved.' But the most celebrated and important of sacred phrases for Sufis is *La 'ilaha 'illa llah*.

Of course, you might recognize this as the first part of the great creedal statement of Islam, the *shahada* (testimony) or *kalimah* (word), also called the *tahlil*, or 'praise.' Literally, it translates to, 'There is no god but God,' which is to say, 'There are no other gods beside *Allah*.'

In the Arabian Peninsula, in the time of the Prophet Muḥammad (ca. 570-632), peace and blessings be upon him, this was a radical statement of monotheism in an otherwise polytheistic tribal culture, advancing the understanding of divinity in that time. It was a unifying idea. Instead of being divided among a host of local deities, associated with this particular river or that particular star, the Arabian tribes now united under one God as one people, saying, 'There is no god but God.'[4]

But, as you might have guessed, Sufis read a still deeper meaning in this phrase, often breaking it into two distinct parts, *La 'ilaha* and *'illa llah*, changing the entire emphasis of the statement.

La 'ilaha means exactly what it says, 'There is no God.' No matter where we look, whether under a microscope or through a telescope, we do not find the God of our Sunday School classes, or our childhood fantasies. God is not hiding under the rug, nor out beyond the stars, like Michelangelo's venerably bearded creator in the Sistine Chapel. In the objective universe, the material universe of science, we do not find God. This is a fact of our experience in the material world. And the Sufi acknowledges this fact, this aspect of our universe, with the declaration, *La 'ilaha,* 'There is no God.'

But that is not where it ends for the Sufi. For the second part of the statement says, *'illa llah,* 'nevertheless, God.' Nevertheless, here in my heart, I have a sense of something sacred, whether I call it 'God' or not. For one person, it may be as simple as an inner longing for 'God,' for something *Greater,* for something *Holy,* or even a transcendent *Possibility;* and for another, it may be an actual experience of holiness, or the sacred, which cannot be proven, but which, at the same time, cannot be un-experienced, or un-known.

Some people say they do not know what 'sacred' means . . . I do not believe them. If you have ever held a newborn child in your hands, or even someone's 'heart' and 'love,' trembling with the responsibility of holding what is too precious to drop, then you know what sacred is. I also think we have many other experiences of profound awareness or mystery throughout our lives that we tend to dismiss, or fail to categorize as 'sacred.'

So while we must concede that, in the world of the senses, there is no observable or demonstrable God; nevertheless, there is often an inner *shahada* or 'testimony' that is continually whispering to us, through a variety of means, *'God.'* This is why the philosopher Martin Buber liked to describe faith as "holy insecurity."[5] It is an insecure knowledge, but a knowledge nonetheless; for while I may not be able to prove it to you, I cannot deny it to myself. It is a sense of something 'holy' which I cannot anchor in external certainty. This is what the statement *La 'ilaha 'illa llah* describes so perfectly, a paradox of subjective and objective experience, or affirmation and negation, the marriage and mingling of two realities.[6]

To this basic statement, *La 'ilaha 'illa llah,* the Sufi often adds the word, *hu.* In Arabic, *hu* literally means 'he'; though, among Sufis, it is, paradoxically, code for the divine feminine, which is to say, the experiential presence of God, the sacred that can be known and felt in experience.[7]

On another level, however, *La 'ilaha 'illa llah,* 'There is no god but God,' is also interpreted by Sufis to mean, 'Nothing exists except divinity.' This is based in an experience confirmed by many Sufis through the centuries, of a unified or unifying wholeness, a sacred substratum to all existence, identified with divinity.

The Chishti-Inayati Zikr

Now every Sufi lineage has its own way of approaching *zikr,* using the sacred phrase, *La 'ilaha 'illa llah hu,* with different melodies, different body movements, and even different pronunciations. In the Inayati lineage of Hazrat Inayat Khan, which is derived from the older Chishti lineage of Central Asia and India, *La 'ilaha 'illa llah hu* is broken into four phrases and four movements that articulate the very paradox we have described, and indeed, the spiritual journey itself.[8]

La 'ilaha—'There is no god.'

Pointing your chin at your left shoulder, you allow your head to loll, drifting down, carried by its own weight and momentum across your chest toward your right shoulder, continuing to arc upward until your face is exposed to the heavens. As your head makes this 270-degree arc, you pronounce the words, *'Lā 'ilāha,'* accompanied by the thought, 'There is no God.'[9]

This is a movement of expansion, of evolution, exploring the material universe, searching for God, and finding only 'Space.' The utterance *La 'ilaha*—'There is no god!' emerges from our throats almost as a plaintive cry. There is a poignancy to the realization, a deep sense of sadness and loss; for we are relational beings, longing to be heard and answered. To search for that God, to cry out and not find God, is a painful experience.[10]

It is at this moment that we feel most lost and bereft. *'There is no God!'* But from the Sufi perspective, it is not *we* who are lost at that moment, but *God* who is lost in the experience of being us! The *kenosis*—the self-emptying of God into us—is so complete at that moment that God cannot be seen through the opacity of a limited self-identity. God is lost, and thus, 'There is no God.'

'Illa—'nevertheless.'

Now, allow your head to fall forward, and your chin to drop straight onto your chest, as you say, *'illa*, 'nevertheless.'[11]

The pain of the external search drives us inward. If there is any value to all the pain we experience in this life, it is this: that it makes us reflective and forces us to look inside ourselves for answers. Our senses naturally take us out. They tell us that everything we want, everything of importance, is outside of ourselves. Having evolved as predators—eyes forward—we learned to think this way, spotting and tracking prey on the horizon. So, in some sense, it was 'natural' for us to look for God and love outside of ourselves, "in all the wrong places," as it were.[12] But the experience of disappointment in this misapprehension leads us to the truth: the thing for which we were searching was always within us, and we begin to ask—'Who am I? What am I about? Why did I do that?'

As the Sufi masters teach us, "To know oneself is to know God."[13]

Llah—'God.'

You now lift your chin off your chest and throw your head back, gently, so you are again facing the heavens. While making this movement, you say, *llah*, 'God!'[14]

Looking within, we find a whole world inside, and begin to discover something of our own, and our own 'God.' It is not the God preached from the pulpit, nor the God of any scripture, but the "God-ideal" of our own making.[15] It is the God-image that reflects and serves our own deepest ideal, and the archetype of our being. It is the 'God' with whom we walk on the journey toward *al-Haqq*, 'God as Truth.'

In the exultation of this discovery within, we lift our heads in inspiration and celebration of what has been discovered—God in our highest ideal![16]

Hu—'Is.'

Now you allow your head to drift slowly and gently down to the left, settling over your heart, as if magnetically drawn there, as you pronounce, *hu.*[17]

The 'God' of our reflection and search within is still only a God-image, an ideal that reflects the state of our own spiritual understanding and development. So where do we discover God in truth? According to Sufism, *in experience*, and experience alone. Through the resonant *hu,* a vibration knocking on the 'door of the heart,' we enter into a relationship with the all-pervasive 'presence'—*huzur.*

Again, having investigated the world in a wide arc, a spiraling and fruitless search for God outside ourselves, we are driven inward by our own disappointment. There, finding something meaningful, something authentic, an ideal within, we ascend the same pole at the center of our being which we have just descended, lifting our heads high, buoyed by the exultation of self-discovery. And yet, this is not actually an experience of divinity, but only a God-image reflecting our ideals. The experience of divinity awaits us yet in the heart.

The Layers of Remembrance

The Chishti-Inayati *zikr* can be practiced silently or out loud. Out loud it is called *zikr jahri.* We do this pronouncing the vowels in the four parts of *La 'ilaha 'illa llah* with aspiration (the exhalation of breath) and a soft lion-like growl.[18]

To keep count, we use a string of ninety-nine beads called a *tesbiḥ,* or 'tool of glorification.' After each segment of thirty-three beads, there is a slightly different counter bead to help us keep track of where we are. The ninety-nine beads are associated with the *'asma al-husna,* the ninety-nine 'beautiful names' of God found in the Qur'an.

Taking up the *tesbiḥ,* we enter into the *zikr* with an invocation, as we mentioned, and begin repeating *La 'ilaha 'illa llah hu* ninety-nine times, slowly, with reverent intention.

Every aspect of the *zikr*—from the specific movements of the body to the most deeply held intention—is truly a prayer in itself; and yet, all work together to build the most complete experience of *zikr.*[19]

Think about it this way . . .

As you start the 'journey,' dropping from your left shoulder and arc-ing over the right, make your movements beautiful, for they are themselves a choreographed prayer to God, illustrating the stages of the spiritual path, drawn like the elegant curves and bold strokes of Arabic calligraphy: the first spiraling movement, the search for God; the second movement, disappointment driving us inward; the third movement, discovery lifting our heads in inspiration; and the fourth movement, settling in the heart where we truly find God.[20] Just making the movements is a prayer in itself articulating our spiritual journey!

Aesthetics are an important element of spiritual practice in Sufism, as it says in the *ḥadith,* "God is beautiful and loves beauty."[21] Thus, performing the movements mindfully, in an aesthetically pleasing way, is already a sign of remembrance, and a pure offering of the body to God.

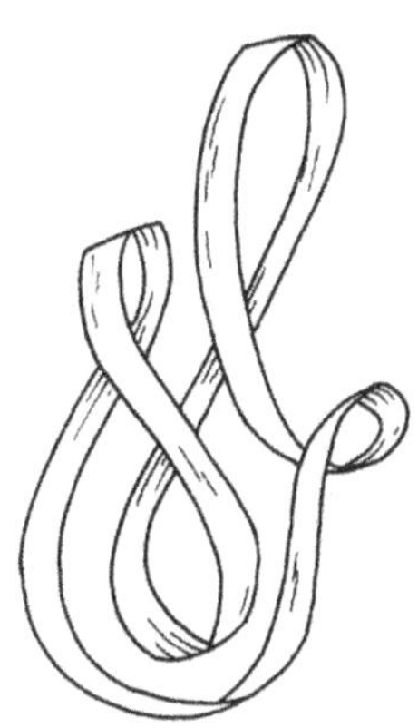

Having established the prayer of the body, you can introduce the prayer of the tongue, *La 'ilaha 'illa llah hu.* This is still better, because now there are actual words of remembrance—with their own sacred vibration, connected to generations of Sufis reciting them through the centuries—upon your lips and entering the atmosphere. And these, too, we can make beautiful, pronouncing them with love and caring attention to their precise pronunciation.[22]

Lā 'ilāha 'illā llāh hū

But it is not long before you discover that the words can easily be said while your mind and attention are wandering off, far into the distance. So, to a simple recitation of the words, we need to add the ingredient of awareness—attention to the words as we are pronouncing them.[23] We need to make it a practice to hear the words we are speaking. Not just to say them; but to hear them, as if spoken to us from without. For we are at least one part of the intended audience for the message of these words.[24]

When that is accomplished and comfortable, we find that we can also add another layer of conscious content to our attention—a layer of intentionality or personal meaning—a private message encoded in the carrier wave of the words.[25] This might be as simple as accompanying the four movements and four parts of the phrase with a personally meaningful translation of the Arabic; for instance, using "There is no God" with *La 'ilaha,* "nevertheless" with *'illa,* "God" with *llah,* and "Is" with *hu.* 'It may not be a literal translation, but it is at least accurate to the intention.

Lā 'ilāha 'illā llāh hū

There is no God; nevertheless, God Is

At this point, having added several layers of content to your *zikr,* it may seem that the practice has become overly complicated, or that it is impossible to maintain an awareness of all these aspects of the *zikr* at once. But remember, every aspect of the *zikr* is good in itself, and an accomplishment not to be discounted. At any given moment, praying the sincere prayer of the body is enough; the careful prayer of the words, enough; the devotion to staying present for God, enough; or the dimension of personal meaning, enough.[26]

The Technology of Remembrance

The ability to hold all aspects of the *zikr* together comes with time, and eventually, the repetition falls into its own rhythms, carrying you into the deepest experience of 'remembrance.'[27]

To use our *tesbiḥ* and repeat a *wazifa,* or mantra, is a purposeful activity that we direct, consciously. It is something that we are doing—'remembering.' But, at a certain point, we may find that we are no longer directing the process consciously, as if something is now being done *to* or *through* us; it is simply 'happening' without conscious intent; that is 'remembrance,' the goal of *zikr* practice.

You may even notice that the mind goes on repeating *La 'ilaha 'illa llah hu* long after the *zikr* is done. This is because *zikr* creates a kind of 'flywheel' in consciousness; once spinning, it continues spinning, even when I rise from my *zikr* and walk out into the world. This is the point and purpose of the practice, to take us from the act of *remembering* to the state of *remembrance,* so that even when I rise from the prayer rug, the phrase, *La 'ilaha 'illa llah hu,* 'There is nothing but divinity,' is still echoing in my head. As Abu Hamid Ghazzali puts it . . .

> Practice this continually, and without interruption; you will reach a point when the motion of the tongue will cease, and it will appear as if the word just flows from it spontaneously. You will go on in this way until every trace of the tongue movement disappears while the heart registers the thought or the idea of the word.[28]

It is as if a 'program' is now operative and running to accomplish its end. It is running when I bump into a co-worker who is rude to me—"There is nothing but divinity.' It is running when I am driving and someone cuts me off in traffic—'There is nothing but divinity.' The substrate awareness, or at least the awareness of the idea—'There is nothing but divinity'—gives us the opportunity to associate it with every person, every object, and every situation we meet, whether apparently 'good' or not. It is like writing the name of God on everything we encounter. If it is God, we may deal with it differently; for remembrance should have implications for our behavior.

Zikr gives us the opportunity to remember our core values, and to sacralize our world, consciously. My co-worker may be mean, but they are still divine. The person who cut me off in traffic may be reckless, but not less sacred because they did so. The question for me is this—'Can I remember the inherent divinity and sacredness of everything in life, no matter what mask God is showing me in the moment?'

Sometimes the answer is, '*Yes,*' sometimes, '*No.*' Sometimes the remembrance does not last very long, and we have to start the wheel spinning again, like an alternator in a car, charging the batteries on our sacred outlook. We do it again and again; and we do it enough throughout our life to transform more and more of our experience of life.[29]

My *murshid* had a favorite Sufi story, a story told of Junayd of Baghdad (835-910) and his favorite disciple, Abu Bakr Shibli (861-946), that illustrates this.

Once, the senior disciples of Junayd came to complain of the apparent favoritism shown to his junior disciple, Shibli, who seemed unworthy of this attention, not being as accomplished or as long with the master as they. In response, Junayd called the disciples together and declared a feast, asking each to go to the market and buy a bird for the stew. With it, they would feed the poor of Baghdad. But when each had returned with a bird for the feast, the master then told each of them to go kill the bird where no one could see and bring it back to the cook.

Following the master's instructions precisely, one disciple closed himself in a closet and killed his bird; another went behind a rock near the river; and still another blindfolded himself, so as not to witness the killing of the bird. In the end, all the disciples had killed their birds and brought them to the cook, except one—Shibli. Feigning anger, Junayd called Shibli before him in the presence of all the disciples and demanded to know why he had not killed the bird as he was told!

Shibli, still holding the bird in his hands, answered mildly: "Master, because I could not find a place where I was not *Seen.*"

Then Junayd looked at the disciples who had complained, as if to say, 'Now, do you see?'

For Shibli, there was no place absent of God, no moment in which he was not aware of God's presence. That is remembrance.[30]

A Temple for the Divine Presence

Pir Vilayat Inayat Khan (1916-2004), the son of Hazrat Inayat Khan, used to talk about traditional Sufi practices as "building a temple for the Divine Presence." Likewise, he said that the Chishti-Inayati form of *zikr*, or 'remembrance' practice, is like "circumambulating the temple."[31]

This is a good way of looking at *zikr* and other Sufi practices in general. These practices help us to make a sacred temple out of this body, sacralizing what we have allowed to become profane, or at least which we have forgotten is inherently holy. In some sense, our practices are done to re-claim and re-dedicate the body as a temple of the divine presence that dwells within it. The particular form of the Chishti-Inayati *zikr* then—with its spiraling movements—is like circumambulating that sacred 'temple' where God dwells in the heart.

Likewise, there is a way of looking at the *zikr* as concentrating and spreading energy, building magnetism in the field around one's body. For the first movement of the *zikr* is creating, as Pir Vilayat put it, a centrifugal force "expanding your consciousness into the galaxies," but also spreading energy, enriching the room in which you do your practice.[32]

This is important, because it is clear that spaces can acquire a definite presence. There are meditation halls I have known that are not simply empty rooms when you walk into them, but rich with a stillness and a quality of peacefulness that can be felt, almost palpably. It is much easier to meditate in such a place, because the atmosphere is already supporting of and conducive to the process and state of meditation. It allows you to drop right into that particular mode.

The first movement of *zikr* builds this magnetism in the field around us. But in the second movement of *zikr*, we are responding to the centripetal forces of our being and the "pull of the center," the solar plexus, "a gate in the center of the centrifuge," where, Pir Vilayat says, "the whole universe gets processed in your being like the water in a lake is processed in the vortex."[33] In the downward and upward movements of the *zikr,* we are connecting to the axis, or pole center of our being, building magnetism near the heart-center.

In the end, there are really two 'temples' created and 'circumambulated' in this practice. One of your own body, and a greater one formed by all of us practicing together—the divine presence dwelling in the space between us. Going around and around, we infuse the temple with the energy of the practice, charging and building a field of energy, saturating the space with our sacred intentions, re-dedicating the temple of the body, and another, greater temple, formed by our communion with each other.

When this is accomplished, we close the ritual very much as we began it, with a dedication. Both hands folded over the heart, we lift the head to the sky and allow it to descend with the words, "This is not my body." Then, turning the head to the left shoulder, we allow it to loll and drift across the chest to the right shoulder, while saying, "This is the temple of God."[34]

In the invocation, at the beginning of our practice, the intention was to go inward. So we said, "This is the temple of the heart." But at the end, as we re-enter the world, we affirm that this body is "The temple of God," dedicated to God and God's service.

silsila

The Chain of Transmission

The Men and Women of Chishti-Inayati Sufism *

The *silsila*, or 'chain' of transmission of a lineage, is of central importance to the Sufi path. It is understood to be a conduit of the *baraka* or spiritual blessing of any genuine Sufi school. It links the murids of an order with the combined spiritual power of their mystical forebears, and with the unseen transformative forces that transpire behind the outward manifestation of this chain or pedigree.

The *silsila* is recited on various occasions, most often before group *zikr*. It is also an important part of the practice known as *tasawwur-i murshid*, in which one works one's way backward through the lineage, connecting with each name or link in the chain, establishing a relationship with each as a spiritual ancestor. In this way, it is likewise connected with Sufi initiation, *bay'ah*, during which it is also sometimes recited. The Arabic word *bay'ah* refers to a covenant sealed by 'taking hand' with another, as the initiate takes the right hand of the Sufi master, a hand that took the hand of the master before, down through the centuries in an unbroken chain. In so doing, the new *murid* may come to realize that this is the hand that took the *actual*

* An edited version of a talk originally given in Boulder, Colorado, on January 11th, 2017, at Naropa University's Sufi Retreat Intensive, and a more developed talk, explicitly proposing a new, integrated Shajara Sharif 'Inayati at the following year's Sufi Retreat Intensive, January 9th, 2018.

hand of another master—whose name, though now famous or even legendary—was nevertheless a real person on the path. This gives the *murid* confidence in what is possible for a human being to achieve.

The Chishti-Nizami-Kalimi Lineage

The *silsila* of Hazrat Pir-o-Murshid Inayat Khan (1882–1927) is that of the Chishti-Nizami-Kalimi lineage, which he inherited from his master, Sayyid Abu Hashim Madani (d. ca.1907), each of the three names—*Chishti-Nizami-Kalimi*—mark a milepost within the lineage, signaling an important emphasis often associated with a person or a place.

Chishti Sufis derive their name from Chisht, a small town in eastern Khurasan (now Afghanistan) near Herat. Sometime in the 10th-century, Khwaja Abu Ishaq Shami (d. 940) was directed by his master, 'Ulu Dinwari in Baghdad, to travel to the far outpost of Chisht, where he initiated a disciple, Khwaja Abu Ahmad Abdal Chishti (d. 966), beginning a succession of masters associated with that humble town.[1] The story told in the lineage of this first Chishti initiation is an interesting one.

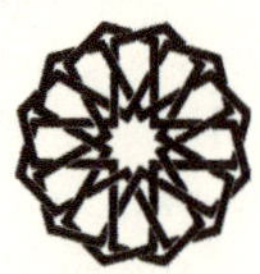

Having traveled to Chisht at the direction of his master, Khwaja Abu Ishaq is first befriended by Ukht Farusnafa, the 'sister of Farusnafa,' who we might call the mother of the Chishtis. A saintly woman of the royal family, the two soon developed a deep spiritual connection.

One day, Khwaja Abu Ishaq confided to his friend, Ukht Farusnafa, that her brother, Emir Farusnafa and his wife would soon have a child. The child he saw would grow up to be a great Sufi; but only if she helped to raise him, imbuing him with her own spiritual blessing. Otherwise, the dissolute ways of his father, the prince, and the temptations of wealth and power, would influence him to evil.

Ukht Farusnafa did as she was asked and became a second mother to her nephew and brother's heir, instilling him with virtues his father did not possess. Over time, he grew into a noble young prince.

One day, while he was out on horseback with a hunting party, he became separated from the others, and his horse soon happened upon a circle of ten Sufis engaged in *zikr*. So struck was he by the sight of these holy beings, and the power radiating from their remembrance of God, that he immediately dismounted and prostrated before them, asking to be admitted to the circle. The leader, Khwaja Abu Ishaq, smiled and initiated Abu Ahmad Abdal, the nephew of his spiritual sister and his long awaited successor.[2]

The Central Asian character of the early Chishti lineage is suggested by use of the title *khwaja* for a number of the early masters of the lineage. Unlike the more familiar titles, *shaykh* or *pir* (meaning, 'elder') used in other regions, the title *khwaja* (master of wisdom) was preferred in Khurasan.[3] Thus, even Mu'in ad-Din Chishti, who brought the Chishti lineage into India, where it took on its distinctive character, was called Khwaja Mu'in ad-Din, as were the four masters who followed him.

Khwaja Mu'in ad-Din (d. 1236) was the disciple of Khwaja 'Usman Harvani (d. 1210), with whom he traveled and served for twenty years, before setting his sights on India late in life.[4] A story of Khwaja Mu'in ad-Din's preaching in India (sometimes told of his master, Khwaja 'Usman Harvani, who did not travel to India) is both entertaining and instructive.

Once in India, Khwaja Mu'in ad-Din quickly attracted thousands of followers, all good Muslims who seemed to be loyal and devoted disciples. But one day, as he was looking out over the masses of them, he suddenly felt he had had enough of all the pomp and said in a voice just loud enough for others to hear, "I think I've changed my mind."

Someone who heard him asked, "Master, about what have you changed your mind?"

"Perhaps," he said, "the Hindus are right, after all . . . I think I must serve the goddess Kali now and make obeisance to her."

The disciple gasped and word quickly spread through the crowd, "The master has become a Hindu and intends to serve the black goddess, Kali!"

Immediately, scores of disciples abandoned him, while others waited to see what he would do next.

Seeing that some disciples still remained, Khwaja Mu'in ad-Din turned in the direction of the local Kali *mandir* (temple) and started to walk.

Seeing this, the remaining disciples deserted him, saying: "How can children of Allah, the formless God, worship the goddess Kali? It is against his own teachings!"

But as he was walking toward the Kali *mandir*, Khwaja Mu'in ad-Din noticed that there was actually one disciple who still remained with him, and he smiled secretly. He was glad to be rid of the others, but if this one had gone, it would have been a real loss. Nevertheless, he continued on toward the temple, thinking about the fickleness of human nature and how quickly the others had departed. He began to pray as he walked, saying—"God! God! What are human beings that you should notice them, when they fail to recognize you in every face before them? You are all and everything!" And with these words, he fell into ecstasy, falling prostrate on the very steps of Kali's temple, facing the statue of Kali!

After he came to, he realized that it must have appeared as if he had made obeisance to Kali, and he said to his only remaining disciple, who was then kneeling beside him and mopping his forehead—"Why do you stay when all the others have left? They're all good Muslims, and there are many learned scholars among them; perhaps you too should go before you are polluted by contact with me."

But the disciple replied, "*Mawla*—master—it was you who taught us that nothing exists except God. And does not the holy Qur'an say, "And wherever you turn, there is God's face." (2:115) If that is true, then Kali is not Kali, and this temple and all of its images are nothing other than divinity. So what does it matter whether you bow to the East or West, to the earth or the heavens? If nothing exists but God, then there is nothing before whom to bow except God, even if one seems to be bowing before Kali."

Then Khwaja Mu'in ad-Din embraced him, and the two departed together. This disciple became his successor, the famous ecstatic, Khwaja Qutb ad-Din.[5]

Khwaja Mu'in ad-Din was called *Gharib Nawaz*, the 'sultan of the poor,' and today, his *dargah* or burial shrine in Ajmer is one of the most important pilgrimage sites in all of India, where thousands of the poor are fed. And yet, it is not Khwaja Mu'in ad-Din's name that is referenced in the trilogy of lineage markers—Chishti-Nizami-Kalimi—but that of Khwaja Nizam ad-Din 'Awliyya (d. 1325), under whom the new Indian form of Chishti Sufism reaches its apogee.

Khwaja Nizam ad-Din, called *Mahbub-i Ilahi*, 'beloved of God,' presided over a court like an ascetic king. Each day, he had hundreds of visitors who left donations which he would then distribute entirely to the poor before retiring at night. Though a wonderful story is also told of a day when he had nothing to give.

Khwaja Nizam ad-Din's most beloved disciple was the poet, Amir Khusraw, who served in the court of the sultan. Once it happened that Amir Khusraw was returning to Delhi after doing some business elsewhere, and stopped to rest at a *caravanserai*, or inn, where he met a man who had just come from Delhi. The man was a farmer who had gone to Delhi after a drought had left him and his family impoverished, hoping that the great saint of Delhi, Khwaja Nizam ad-Din, would help him. Khwaja Nizam ad-Din always gave whatever he had, but it happened that on that day, no donations had been received, so nothing could be given. But Nizam ad-Din could not bear to turn the farmer away empty-handed, so he gave the barefoot farmer his own sandals, which he had received from his master, Baba Farid. The farmer, who had hoped for money or food, accepted the sandals with quiet disappointment.

Later, when the farmer encountered Amir Khusraw and recounted these events, the poet's eyes lit up and he exclaimed, "Do you mean to say that you are in possession of the holy sandals of Khwaja Nizam ad-Din?"

The farmer produced the sandals, and Amir Khusraw immediately produced a chest of gold and offered to trade. The farmer was beside himself with happiness, and so was Amir Khusraw.

A few days later, Amir Khusraw arrived in Delhi, bearing Khwaja Nizam ad-Din's sandals on his head.

Khwaja Nizam ad-Din asked, "How much did you pay for those sandals?"

"All that I possess," he replied.

And Khwaja Nizam ad-Din said with a smile, "You bought them cheaply!"[6]

Khwaja Nizam ad-Din was the twentieth master in the lineage after the prophet Muḥammad, peace and blessings be upon him. In the thirtieth generation came Shah Kalim Allah Jahanabadi (1650-1729), a grandson of the architect of the Taj Mahal and Lal Qila, who himself would become one of the great architects of the lineage, initiating a renaissance in Chishti Sufism.[7]

A resident of Delhi, Shah Kalim Allah's home near Lal Qila, the famous 'Red Fort,' became the principal seat of the Chishti lineage in the Mughal Period. A gifted intellectual and leader, he sought "to reunify the many regional Chishti centers and emphasize the core teachings of the original Chishti lineage."[8]

One aspect of this reunification and revival was achieved through his writings, such as his classic work, *Kashkul-i Kalimi,* 'The Alms-bowl of Kalim,' in which he gathered and collected teachings on meditation and contemplation from numerous Sufi masters for the benefit of his students and future Sufis of the Chishti lineage.[9]

But Shah Kalim Allah also seems to have been unusually broad-minded; for unlike many Sufi masters, he initiated both men and women, Muslims and non-Muslims alike.[10] And despite his abiding commitment to the Chishti lineage (to which he gave primary allegiance), he actually carried the transmission of all four of the early schools of Sufism— Chishti, Naqshbandi, Qadiri, and Suhrawardi—and thus, the Kalimi lineage which stems from him, has sometimes been called the lineage of "Four-School Sufism."[11]

The four schools had begun their unification with the Chishti-Nizami master, Shaykh Mahmud Rajan (d. 1495), who also carried the Suhrawardi transmission, and was continued by Shaykh Hasan Muḥammad (d. 1575), who carried the Qadiri transmission, until finally being unified by Shah Kalim Allah, as a carrier of the Naqshbandi transmission.[12] Thus, it was a characteristic of masters within the Kalimi lineage to emphasize training in the teachings and practices of all four schools.

Shah Kalim Allah himself had directed his successor, Shaykh Nizam ad-Din Awrangabadi (d. 1730), to emphasize the teaching of whichever school might best suit those to whom he was guiding; for he recognized that the needs of the seeker are paramount, and each must be given the particular nourishment they require.[13]

Almost two hundred years later, Hazrat Inayat Khan would confirm this emphasis of the Kalimi lineage, writing in his *Confessions* of the training he had received from his own master, Sayyid Abu Hashim Madani . . .

> I studied the Qur'an, Hadith, and the literature of the Persian mystics. [...] After receiving instruction in the five different grades of Sufism, the physical, intellectual, mental, moral, and spiritual, I went through a course of training in the four schools: the Chishti, Naqshbandi, Qadiri, and Suhrawardi.[14]

The Four-School Sufism of Shah Kalim Allah, and his open attitude toward the initiation of women and non-Muslims, would in time become foundational aspects of Hazrat Inayat Khan's universalist Sufism.

The Women of the Chishti Lineage

The thirty-seven names and lives that comprise the traditional Chishti-Nizami-Kalimi *silsila,* or chain of transmission—from the prophet Muḥammad to Hazrat Inayat Khan—span almost 1,400 years of spiritual blessing. Some of the names, like Hasan of Basra, Ibrahim ibn Adham and Mu'in ad-Din Chishti, are famous among all Sufis, their sayings and deeds recorded in classic texts and remembered throughout the Sufi world. Some, like Qutb ad-Din Bakhtiyar Kaki, Farid ad-Din Ganj-i Shakkar, Nizam ad-Din 'Awliyya, and Nasir ad-Din Chiragh-i Delhi, are more famous within the Chishti lineage. And some names are so obscure, even within the lineage, that we know almost nothing about them.

Sadly, we know even less about the many women who have influenced the lineage. And yet, we live in a time that demands a more balanced perspective. If the *silsila* is meant to connect us with the flow of blessing in our tradition, and to inspire confidence in it, we must see ourselves represented in it, women as well as men.

For many women, the *silsila* is no longer inspiring. A long list of exclusively male names, however great and holy, is not necessarily meaningful to the many gifted women who often make up the majority of universalist Sufi circles today. The message, whether intentional or merely the inertial effect of historical patriarchy, is one of exclusion. "Where are the women?" we hear, which is another way of saying, "Where do I fit in this tradition?"

One answer is that women have always been present in Sufism, which is true. Accounts of women saints are found throughout Sufi literature; indeed, many of them are found in the writings of one of the greatest medieval Sufi masters, Muhyiddin ibn 'Arabi, as he describes the great women Sufis with whom he learned in Al-Andalus.[15] Likewise, in the 17th-century, the famous Sufi Mughal prince, Dara Shikuh, included a section on "wise, virtuous, perfected, and united" women in his *Safinat al-Awliyya'*, 'ship of saints.'[16] And few Sufis are more acclaimed than Rabi'a al-Adawiyya of Basra, who is credited by most as changing the emphasis of Sufism toward divine love.[17]

But even the great Rabi'a of Basra is not included in any Sufi *silsila,* and her example, though profound, is but one shining exception among hundreds of male saints. So where are the women? we ask again. The answer is uncomfortably obvious—silent and silenced by patriarchal culture, buried in the footnotes of history. The vast majority of women throughout Sufi history have not had the same opportunity for spiritual pursuits as men, and even when they did, they were often illiterate and their sayings rarely recorded by their male counterparts. Those who were literate, usually belonging to the most privileged classes, existed in another type of cage, like Princess Jahanara, the sister of Dara Shikuh, who was not allowed by precedent or prejudice to inherit the lineage of her male teacher, even though he wished it.[18]

With few exceptions, that was simply the reality. But there is nothing to say that we need to be satisfied with that reality. In recent years, many have begun the work of reclaiming the legacy of Sufi women.[19] For the women of the Chishti lineage, we can do the same; though it is difficult work, and often the results yield less of a picture of these women than we might desire. And yet it must be done.

It requires a deep knowledge of the Chishti literature, and an ability to access the historical sources. Today, the foremost expert in the history of the *silsila*, and the sources of information regarding it, is our own beloved companion on the path, Pir Zia Inayat-Khan—Sarafil Bawa. In two separate works, he has given us the gift of an otherwise unobtainable portrait of the Chishti lineage in the English language: a scholarly treatment in "The 'Silsila-i Sufian': From Khwaja Mu'in al-Din Chishti to Sayyid Abu Hashim Madani," found in the edited volume, *A Pearl in Wine: Essays on the Life, Music and Sufism of Hazrat Inayat Khan*; and a less formal oral presentation of Chishti lore, edited by us both, in *Tree of Lights: The Chishti Lineage of Hazrat Inayat Khan.*[20]

Through these works, the wisdom of generations of Sufis in the Chishti-Nizami-Kalimi *silsila* has become accessible to English speaking Sufis, and we begin to see the faces of women connected with the *silsila* peeking through the latticework of history, some playing prominent roles in the shaping of the lineage.

In some cases, we do not know their names. They are simply—Ukht Farusnafa, 'sister of Farusnafa,' who we have already called the "mother of the Chishtis"; Umm Abu Muḥammad, the 'mother of Abu Muḥammad,' "a woman of extraordinary insight and wisdom," who gave her son his first teachings in Sufism;[21] Zawja Bakhtiyar Kaki, 'wife of the One Who is Fortunate in Bread,' who is connected with a miracle;[22] or Ukht Chiragh-i Dehli, the 'sister of the Lamp of Dehli,' the sister and mother of Chishti masters.[23]

But many names are known—names like, Bibi Safiyya, Bibi Amat al-Ghani, Sayyid Begum, or Muhtarima Poti Begum Sahiba. The words *bibi, muhtarima,* and *sahiba* are titles of respect, generally meaning, 'lady.' And *begum* is a married woman of high rank. Though, in many cases, we know little more of them than their relationship to one of the lineage masters, or for instance, that Shaykh 'Ilm ad-Din's mother, Bibi Safiyya, was a granddaughter of a Sufi saint called "The Ocean-Drinker," and was herself "A soulful woman possessed of unique powers of insight."[24]

In another class are those who, whether their names are known or not, play a significant part in a story or anecdote in the lineage, or are themselves Sufis of note. These include—Bibi Hafiza Jamal, the daughter of Khwaja Mu'in ad-Din, who had memorized the entire Qur'an, and who was so gifted spiritually that her father actually made her one of his successors;[25] Bibi Zulaykha, the saintly mother of Khwaja Nizam ad-Din, of whom it is said, "Every month when the Shaykh saw the new moon, he offered felicitation to his mother by placing his head at her feet," and whenever he had a problem after her death, went to pray at her grave;[26] and Bibi Fatimah Sam, a great Sufi saint of Delhi.

The latter was revered by both Khwaja Farid ad-Din and Khwaja Nizam ad-Din. When discussing the place of women saints in Sufism, and talking about Bibi Fatimah Sam, Khwaja Nizam ad-Din said, "When a wild lion comes into the city from the forest, who asks whether it is male or female?"[27] He even told stories of her on more than one occasion and quoted verses attributed to her . . .

For love you search, while still for life you strain.
For both you search, but both you can't attain.[28]

Ultimately, love leaves no room for the self, says Bibi Fatimah Sam.

And then there are the great ladies of Islam and Sufism who are connected with the Chishti lineage—Khadijah al-Kubra, 'A'ishah Umm al-Mu'minin, and Umm Salama, the wives of the prophet Muḥammad; Fatimah az-Zahra, the daughter of the Prophet; Rabi'a al-Basri, who changed the course of Sufism; and Shahzadi Jahanara Begum Sahiba (1614-1681), the daughter of the Mughal emperor, Shah Jahan.

Though a disciple of a Qadiri master, Mulla Shah, Princess Jahanara later had a profound mystical experience while on pilgrimage at the burial shrine of Khwaja Mu'in ad-Din Chishti (on whom she wrote a biography), 'taking hand' with the sainted Chishti master in the inner world some four centuries after his death.[29] She is buried near the *dargah* of Khwaja Nizam ad-Din, and upon her simple marble marker is written . . .

He is the Living, the Sustaining.
Let no one cover my grave except with greenery,
For this grass suffices as a tomb cover for the poor.
The annihilated faqir *Lady Jahanara,*
Disciple of the Lords of Chisht,
Daughter of Shahjahan the Warrior
(may God illuminate his proof).[30]

The Integrated Shajara Sharif 'Inayati

As we have seen, the *silsila* traces initiatic ancestry from one master to another, rather than the full flow of *baraka* or spiritual blessing from all of the figures, male and female, that have influenced its direction and development. If we would see something of this greater influence, we must look to the *shajara* of the lineage.

The graphic representation of the *silsila* is called the *shajara sharif*, or 'noble tree.' The *shajara* of Hazrat Pir-o-Murshid

Inayat Khan is the Shajara Sharif 'Inayati. This tree traces the Chishti-Nizami-Kalimi lineage imparted to him by his master before his passing. The addition of 'Inayati' marks his own contribution as the opener of the way of universalist Sufism.

Although the *shajara sharif* is usually a simple linear list of the names of the *silsila* masters, there is no necessity of its being limited to this simple form. In the *shajara*, we have the possibility of seeing more complexity. The *silsila* may be fixed in the historical reality of how the lineage was passed from one male master to another, but the *shajara* can also show us the missing women of the lineage, filling out the leaves and branches that would illustrate its full majesty.

Of course, we must acknowledge the fact that, according to historical circumstances beyond our control, or even the control of those who came before us, the *silsila* was forged and passed on in the form it was, from one male successor to another for nearly 1,400 years. But we can also begin to acknowledge the women who influenced and impacted the lineage through the centuries in our *shajara*, doing what we can to reclaim their legacy of service and sacrifice, adding their names to the ancestral tree of the lineage.

Thus, a new, integrated Shajara Sharif 'Inayati has been created to bring the men and women of the lineage together for the first time.[31]

Hazrat Inayat Khan himself said, "I see as clear as daylight that the hour is coming when women will lead humanity to a higher evolution."[32] And still more significantly, he granted the rank of *murshid* to only four disciples in his lifetime, all of them women: Murshida Rabia Martin (1871-1947), Murshida Sharifa Goodenough (1876-1937), Murshida Sophia Saintsbury-Green (1866-1939), and Murshida Fazal Mai Egeling (1861-1939). But for various reasons, none of these women have ever been represented in the shajaras of the many lineages of Inayati Sufism. However, today we must acknowledge their place as the mothers of Inayati Sufism who preceded and gave their blessing to all the lineage masters who came after them.

For this reason, the integrated Shajara Sharif 'Inayati gives them their proper place beneath the name of Hazrat Pir-o-Murshid Inayat Khan, prior to the branching of the universalist Sufi lineage into its many current expressions.

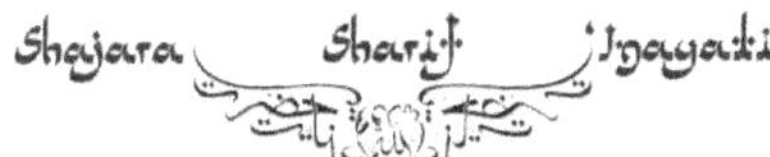

Khadijah al-Kubra + Hazrat Muhammad, Rasul Allah + 'A'ishah, Umm al-Mu'min

Umm Salama + Hazrat 'Ali, Wali Allah + Fatimah az-Zahra

Hazrat Khwaja Rabi'a Basri + Hazrat Khwaja Hasan Basri

Hazrat Khwaja 'Abd al-Wahid bin Zayd

Hazrat Khwaja Fuzayl bin 'Ayaz

Hazrat Khwaja Ibrahim ibn Adham Balkhi

Hazrat Khwaja Huzayfa Mar'ashi

Hazrat Khwaja Hubayra Basri

Hazrat Khwaja Mumshad 'Ulu Dinwari

Ukht Farusnafa + Hazrat Khwaja Abu Ishaq Shami Chishti

Umm Abu Muhammad + Hazrat Khwaja Abu Ahmad Abdal Chishti

Hazrat Khwaja Abu Muhammad Chishti

Hazrat Khwaja Nasir ad-Din Abu Yusuf Chishti

Hazrat Khwaja Qutb ad-Din Mawdud Chishti

Hazrat Khwaja Hajji Sharif Zindani

Hazrat Khwaja 'Usman Harvani

Hazrat Khwaja Mu'in ad-Din Hasan, Gharib Nawaz

Bibi Hafiza Jamal + Hazrat Khwaja Qutb ad-Din Mas'ud, Bakhtiyar Kaki + Zawja Bakhtiyar Kaki

Bibi Sharifa + Hazrat Khwaja Farid ad-Din Mas'ud, Ganj-i Shakar

Bibi Zulaykha + Hazrat Khwaja Nizam ad-Din Auliya', Mahbub-i Ilahi + Bibi Fatimah Sam

Ukht Chiragh-i Delhi + Hazrat Khwaja Nasir ad-Din Mahmud, Chiragh-i Delhi

Hazrat Shaykh al-Mashaykh Kamal ad-Din 'Allama

Bibi Safiya + Hazrat Shaykh al-Mashaykh Siraj ad-Din, Siraj al-Auliya'

Bibi Maryam + Hazrat Shaykh al-Mashaykh 'Ilm ad-Din

Malik Bibi + Hazrat Shaykh al-Mashaykh Mahmud Rajan + Bibi Man Sahiba

Bibi Khadijah + Hazrat Shaykh al-Mashaykh Jamal ad-Din Jamman

Bibi Amat al-Ghani + Hazrat Shaykh al-Mashaykh Hasan Muhammad

Bibi Khadijah + Hazrat Shaykh al-Mashaykh Muhammad A'zam + Bibi 'A'ishah

Jahanara Begum Sahib, Faqira + Hazrat Shaykh al-Mashaykh Yahya Madani + Amat-i Sattar

Hazrat Shaykh al-Mashaykh Shah Kalim Allah Jahanabadi

Sayyid Begum + Hazrat Shaykh al-Mashaykh Nizam ad-Din Aurangabadi

Hazrat Shaykh al-Mashaykh Maulana Fakhr ad-Din

Hazrat Shaykh al-Mashaykh Ghulam Qutb ad-Din

Hazrat Shaykh al-Mashaykh Ghulam Nasir ad-Din Mahmud, Kale Miyan

Muhtarima Poti Begum Sahiba + Hazrat Shaykh al-Mashaykh Muhammad Hasan Jili Kalimi

Hazrat Shaykh al-Mashaykh Sayyid Muhammad Abu Hashim Madani

Pirani Ameena Begum + Hazrat Pir-o-Murshid 'Inayat Khan + Pirzadi Noor-un-Nisa Inayat Khan

Murshida Rabia Martin + Murshida Sharifa Goodenough + Murshida Sophia Saintsbury-Green + Murshida Fazal Mai Egeling

kalimat-i qudsiyya

Eight Principles of Sufi Mindfulness

The Sacred Words of the Masters of Wisdom *

Once, on a pilgrimage to the grave of Khwaja Mu'in ad-Din Chishti in Ajmer, a young Hazrat Inayat Khan rose in the middle of the night to pray. As dawn approached, he heard the song of a wandering dervish come drifting through his window . . .

> *'Awake! Awake from your sleep!*
> *Death awaits us in every moment.*
> *You've no idea the burden you've gathered,*
> *Nor how long the journey!*
> *Get up! Up! The night is passing and the sun rising!'*[1]

In the profound stillness of the hour, seated on his prayer rug with beads in hand, the message of the song stirred and moved the young Inayat Khan to tears. Suddenly, he rose and walked out of his hotel. Lost in thought and walking aimlessly, he came unexpectedly to a cemetery where he saw a group of dervishes seated on the grass. Though dressed in rags, he was astonished to see that they treated one another like royalty, with courtly manners. Just then, another group approached. It was their

* An edited version of a talk given in New Lebanon, New York, on April 4th, 2017, at the Abode of the Message "Traditions Class," and earlier talks in Boulder, Colorado, on January 10th, 2017, at Naropa University, and in the Boulder Sufi community, ca. 2013.

murshid, accompanied by more dervishes who walked before him like heralds, crying out—*Hosh dar dam! Nazar bar qadam! Safar dar vatan! Khilvat dar anjuman!*—'Be conscious of your breath! Watch every step! Journey homeward! Solitude in the crowd!'[2]

It was the anthem of the Sufis.

There is a traditional Sufi admonition I like, something Sufis say to one another to remind themselves of their roots and their ideals.

Once Sufism was a reality without a name;
now it is but a name without a reality.[3]

It is as if to say—'Once, we didn't even know what to call ourselves; but the spirit was real among us and we did the *work.* Name or no name; it didn't matter. Now we call ourselves *Sufis,* carry beads and wear the dervish cloak; but where is the work, where is the spirit?' It is a check on external Sufism, getting caught-up in the name and form, while forgetting the essence.

We are called 'Sufis' today because once we were laughed at and derided for wearing rough wool *(suf)* and living ascetic lives on the margins of society, so that we came to be called, jokingly, *sufiyya,* the 'wool-wearers.' But that is only the name that stuck. In the earliest period of Sufism, Sufis were called by various names, including *nussak* (ascetics), *'arifun* (gnostics), *hukama* (wise), and in one part of Central Asia, *khwajaghan,* or 'masters of wisdom.'

The Khwajaghan were a loosely identified group of 'Sufis' who developed a distinctive body of teachings and practices that continue to inspire and challenge Sufis to this day.

The masters among them were not called *shaykh* or *murshid*, 'elder' or 'guide,' as they are today, but *khwaja*, 'wise one.'[4] It is a title that appears in the early tradition of at least two of the great schools of Sufism, the Chishti and Naqshbandi lineages.

This Chishti lineage was originally a Central Asian lineage, and may have had some connection with those we call the Khwajaghan, as all the masters of the lineage up to Khwaja Nasir ad-Din Chiragh-i Delhi, the 'lamp of Delhi,' bear this title. Nevertheless, the Khwajaghan are most associated with the pre-history of the Naqshbandi lineage, which explicitly honors and carries their distinctive emphasis.

The Khwajaghan were serious in their practice and held a no-nonsense attitude to external forms. They dressed as ordinary people, blending in, drawing very little attention to themselves, just doing 'the work.' They did that work in the world, like everyone else, but while also holding an internal center and focus on the sacred.[5]

It is said that they would have preferred that Mansur al-Hallaj be more sober, more circumspect in his outward behavior, saying in essence: 'What need is there to show your ecstasy in public? Saying *An al-Haqq—I am the Truth* in front of people who are likely to misunderstand you? You'll just draw attention to yourself, and to us; we don't need that kind of attention.'[6]

The Khwajaghan may have also been influenced by the surviving elements of Buddhism in Central Asia, as there were still Buddhist monasteries present in this period. We say this because the teachings of the Khwajaghan are somewhat different from those of other Sufis, and even their language seems to reflect some Buddhist influence: they spoke of the goal of the path as *itlaq*, 'liberation,' a term little used by other Sufis; and they spoke less about *Allah*, and more about the divine reality, *al-Haqq*, 'the Truth.'[7]

The Sacred Words

Among the greatest masters of the Khwajaghan is Khwaja 'Abd al-Khaliq Ghujdawani (d.1179). The chief disciple of the grandmaster, Khwaja Yusuf Hamadani (1062-1141), Ghujdawani was considered the "chief custodian of the Tradition,"[8] and articulated the basic principles of practice and the path among the Khwajaghan—the *kalimat-i qudsiyya,* the eight principles of Sufi mindfulness that became foundational for the Naqshbandi lineage.

The *kalimat-i qudsiyya,* or 'sacred words,' are equivalent to what might be called sutras in the Indian Hindu and Buddhist traditions. That is to say, they are boiled-down, aphoristic statements, easily memorized, that use as few words as possible to convey a deep principle which may be unpacked later by a knowledgeable master. In this case, eight foundational principles in Arabic and Farsi that outline the essence of the Sufi path, as well as the Sufi meditative process.

1. Hosh dar dam – 'Mind on the Breath!'

The first of the eight principles is *hosh dar dam,* 'mind on the breath,' or 'awareness on the breath.'

Why is the breath so important? In his *Fawatih al-Jamal,* the great Sufi master Najm ad-Din Kubra (1145-1221) points out the secret of the name *Allah.* Of course, we know the name *Allah* is probably a contraction of the Arabic definite article *al-* and *ilah,* making *'The God.'* But Najm ad-Din Kubra reminds us that *Allah* is made up of four letters—*'alif-lam-lam-ha'*. The *'alif* and the first *lam* are the definite article in Arabic, *al-* or 'the.' But when you put two of the same letter together in Arabic, as we have with *lam-lam,* it signals an intensification of meaning related to what follows. In this case, the aspirated *ha'*, which is symbolic of and sounds like the breath as we exhale it, *ha-a-a-h.*

Thus, *Allah* is *'The very breath,'* the subtle essence that pervades and connects all being! This is God.[9]

Therefore, we are never closer to God than when we are aware of our breath, and never more distant than when we forget it. Indeed, Sayyid Abu Hashim Madani tells us, "There is only one virtue and one sin; to breathe in remembrance of God, or to breathe a single breath in forgetfulness."[10]

Likewise, Khwaja 'Abd al-Khaliq Ghujdawani says, "Every breath inhaled and exhaled with heedlessness is dead, disconnected from the Divine Presence."[11] This is because the letter *ha'* is also a feminine "sound figure" in Arabic that suggests "spirit," like the Arabic word *hu* or *huwa,* a similarly aspirated word which we, as Sufis, associate with the divine presence.[12]

The sound of the *huwa,* and the secret of the divine name, *Allah,* says Najm ad-Din Kubra, is flowing through our bodies with every inhalation and exhalation, obedient to the divine will, even if we are ignorant of it. Thus, awareness of the breath's deep significance, is a redemptive act, connecting us with divinity.[13]

Of course, it is not the physical breath itself that is of such great importance here, but the message it carries—the subtle essence, the *prana* or *nafas batin* for which the physical breath is only a carrier wave. That is the deeper divine essence and the active ingredient in all our intentionality. It is in our cells and pervades everything in us, and all being. Thus, 'consciousness on the breath' points to the metaphysical teaching that God is the very essence of our being.

And yet, it is also a simple instruction—'Pay attention to your breath and see what happens.'

Try closing your eyes and observing your breath as it enters and leaves your nostrils, touching the fine hairs that surround them. Observe what it does to consciousness when you bring your attention to the breath entering and leaving your body, for "Breath is the foundation of this path," says Khwaja Baha' ad-Din Naqshband.[14]

2. *Nazar bar qadam* – 'Watch Your Step!'

The second principle is *nazar bar qadam,* 'watch your step.'

In terms of the larger path, *nazar bar qadam* is clear: literally and figuratively, 'Watch your step!'

Nazar bar qadam is a total awareness of your actions, watchfulness over everything you do.[15] What kind of words are you using? What does your behavior look like? What kind of company do you keep? What kind of life are you leading? How have you ordered your life? Is it ordered to accomplish your goals, or is it ordered to accomplish something entirely contrary to those goals? Pay attention—watch your step, and "Direct yourself constantly toward your goal."[16]

But it is also a practical instruction: literally, watch your step. For the Khwajaghan, it was a practice to lower the gaze, looking down at the feet in an attitude of humility. It was another way of saying, 'Be careful where you cast your eyes; they can lead you astray!'

Whatever we look upon reflects on the mirror of the heart;

it leaves an impression there, and stimulates a response in us. "The gaze precedes the step and the step follows the gaze," says Shaykh Ahmad Sirhindi. Thus, Sufis would look down so as not to take in unhelpful impressions.[17]

In a slightly different vein, Khwaja Baha' ad-Din Naqshband would also say, "If we look at the mistakes of our friends, we will be left friendless, because no one is perfect."[18] Here the emphasis is on keeping our gaze directed at ourselves, on the direction of our own steps, always noting the imperfect "beam" in our own eye before judging the "mote" in the eye of another. (Matt. 7:3-5) This is the proper focus.

According to G.I. Gurdjieff's disciple, J.G. Bennett, *qadam* derives from the tri-literal Semitic root *q-d-m*, "which expresses source or origin." Thus, *nazar bar qadam* can also be interpreted to mean, "Remember where you came from and where you are going. Keep your attention on the step you are taking at this moment."[19] This is directly connected to the Sufi metaphor of the *suluk*, the 'journey.' Thus, a Sufi is also called a *salik*, a 'traveler,' one who walks the spiritual path. But this is also meant literally, as Sufis traditionally undertake pilgrimages, traveling from place to place in search of spiritual guidance, including the guidance that comes from the contemplative experience of walking itself, as Thoreau suggests in his famous essay on walking.[20]

When the *salik* walks, they watch their steps, undistracted from the goal of their journey.[21] And just as there is an almost Buddhist orientation to breath awareness in *hosh dar dam*, there is likewise a suggestion of actual walking meditation in *nazar bar qadam*. Indeed, the two may be coordinated, just as they are in Buddhist practice, walking with a specific breathing rhythm.

For Sufis, walking meditation takes a somewhat different form than it does for Buddhists. The walking meditation of Buddhism is very slow and deliberate, focusing awareness on the action of lifting one foot very slowly on the inhalation and bringing it down equally slowly on the exhalation, step after step in conscious succession.

In contrast, Sufi walking meditation tends to emphasize a normal walking rhythm, often on a four count, using the phrase, *La 'ilaha 'illa llah.*

Inhaling to a count of four, one takes four steps, starting with the right foot, remembering each of the four parts of the phrase *La 'ilaha 'illa llah* with each of the four footfalls. The same sequence is then repeated with the exhalation, going on continuously, inhaling and exhaling the phrase to a count of four throughout one's walk.[22]

Because this is a *fikr,* or 'contemplation' practice, placing the phrase silently on the breath, it can be done anywhere, in any circumstance, adjusting easily to the situation without drawing any attention to the *salik.* No one would even know that you are 'being spiritual'—a great drawback to the practice for some.

Another version of Sufi walking meditation, however, is simply to bring your consciousness very close to your nostrils as you breathe and walk.

Imagine you are walking, eyes open, with your awareness 'drawn back,' near the opening of your nostrils as you breathe. In this way, awareness stays close to the body, instead of wandering out into the distance, as it usually does with the eyes, looking for movement and specific objects of interest. The eyes are still open in this meditation, but they are not looking for 'entertainment.' They see trees and tree branches approaching, people and other shapes coming toward them, but your awareness is actually near the nostrils with your breath the whole time.

Doing this practice, we experience the world differently from how we ordinarily experience it. Walking with our awareness on the breath at our nostrils—neither particularly fast nor slow—creates an effect we sometimes see in a video, when the camera moves through a landscape or a crowd of people, and everything seems to be coming toward us, moving passed or around us.

When you bring your attention to the breath entering and exiting your body at the very edge of your nostrils, to the sensation of the tiny, almost cilia-like hairs that cover our entire body, feeling the air move them, you experience the world differently. You experience the tree branch as it comes up to greet you, moving on just as naturally and seamlessly—this person or that person, this building or that, all greeting us and gently moving on.

On the other hand, when awareness is 'out there,' with the eyes, life is perceived more like a screen on which images are projected. It is less relational somehow, and more an entertainment of the mind.

3. Safar dar vatan – 'Journey Homeward!'

The third principle is *safar dar vatan*, 'journey homeward,' or 'journey in your homeland.'

In the Abrahamic traditions, we have specific words for 'returning home,' or 'turning back to God.' They are the same words used for 'repentance.' In Hebrew, the word is *t'shuvah.* In Arabic, it is *tawba.* And in Greek, it is *metanoia.* But they all carry the same basic meaning, 'turning around.' Repentance has the sense of *mea culpa*, 'It's my fault,' or 'I'm guilty.' But *t'shuvah, tawba,* and *metanoia* only mean 'turning' or 'turning back.'

From the time we are born, we begin a walk out into life. We stumble forward, compelled by the gravity pull of our basic drives and the world's expectations. But at a certain point, we come into an awareness that we can actually make a choice, or that we may need to live our lives on purpose now, with a definite intention. Often it is because we have been hurt in our wanderings, or have hurt others. It is at this point that we may want to 'turn it around,' turning back to the source and center of our being. We have the sense that we have wandered far from where we needed to be, and it is now time to 'turn around' and 'journey homeward.'

For the Sufi, this is a journey from the "world of appearances to the World of Reality,"[23] from the world of "unrealized potential" in conventional reality "to the world of will, *alam-i wujub,*" where we become aware of our destiny and our ability to fulfill it.[24] It is a journey from "blameworthy to praiseworthy" human qualities.[25]

And yet, *safar dar vatan* is more properly translated, 'journey *in* your homeland.' It suggests that we need to see what we think we already know with fresh eyes, to look at our world from a new perspective, seeing what we have hitherto failed to recognize. According to the Naqshbandis, it is a reference to the internal journey, the exploration to be made inside each one of us.[26] Take the journey inward and find out what is going on with you.

We are constantly taking an external journey away from home. Our senses lead us out all the time. They tell us that everything we want, everything of importance is outside of ourselves; but they are wrong. 'Who am I? What am I about? Why did I do that?' These are questions that can only be answered on the inward journey, on the pilgrimage to the *ka'bah* of the heart.

4. *Khilvat dar anjuman* – 'Solitude in the Crowd!'

When Khwaja Baha' ad-Din Naqshband was asked to give over the basic principle of spiritual development, he said, "*Khilvat dar anjuman*, 'solitude in the crowd,' being outwardly with people, but inwardly with God."[27]

The fourth principle is to meditate in the midst of a crowd, to be able to hold your internal center amid the noise of the world, and not be constantly moved by it.

We think we are sovereign human beings, making our own choices in this world; but are we really? Imagine I am walking downtown and some young man brushes into me, walks right into my shoulder on purpose, as if to tell me I am *'in his space,'* trying to intimidate me. Well, the macho kid in me that grew up 'in the neighborhood,' knows exactly what is meant by this, and goes into a reptilian fight mode. I turn, angrily, ready to confront him. But just then, unexpectedly, I find myself facing the woman I love. *Where did she come from?* It turns out she had seen me walking and come over just as the boy brushed into me. She kisses me, and now I am happy beyond belief, wrapped in the warmth of my feelings for her. We start to talk and reconnect when another man, not paying attention to where he is going, stumbles into us both, accidentally knocking her forward and stepping on my toe! Again, I am angry, but now for another reason!

It is exactly as if I were a leaf blown by every wind!

This is what so much of our lives are like: I'm hungry, so I'm irritable. I eat something and feel better. Now I can be nice again. Someone is rude to me at work, so it's a 'bad day.' Someone gives me an unexpected gift on the way home and suddenly it's a 'good day.' . . . One reaction after another.

At some point, we have to ask ourselves—'Is there any *me* to *me?* Where am *I* in all of these reactions? Am I anything but a set of preferences and judgments? Is this *life* anything but a series of pre-programmed responses to so-called 'good' and 'bad' events? Is this what it is to be human? What part of a human being is sovereign and independent if it is always in a state of reactivity?'

I respond to pleasure with happiness. I respond to pain with unhappiness.

The Sufi wants to know if it is possible to be something different; is it possible to have a different response? Can I still be happy or calm if somebody steps on my toe or hurts my feelings?

We have the capacity to be something different; but will we? Is it really a 'bad day' because it rained and so-and-so didn't call me? Or did it simply rain on a day when no one called?

Khilvat dar anjuman, 'solitude in the crowd,' is finding and holding an internal center amid all the distractions of life, finding a sovereign response amid all the pre-programmed reactions available to us. It is being "free from limitation in the midst of limitations," as the modern Turkish Sufi master, Hasan Lufti Shushud, put it.[28] Whatever is going on outside, we want to "remain inwardly free,"[29] entering "fully into the life of the external world without losing" our internal freedom.[30]

Having taken the journey inward, then—"in the homeland"—discovering who you are, apart from reactions and reactivity—you learn to hold a center in the midst of the crowd. It is not necessary to be blown by every wind; there is a human possibility beyond reactivity which holds the key to our most authentic identity.

In terms of practice around *khilvat dar anjuman*, the Sufi masters make a distinction between external solitude and internal solitude, *khalwah zahirah* and *khalwah batinah*, the former being a physical retreat from the world, and the latter the internal retreat in the cell of the heart.[31] "The aim of the external solitude is the attainment of internal solitude," the last rung on the ladder leading to union with God.[32]

5. *Yad Kard* – 'Remembering!'

The fifth of the eight principles is *yad kard,* 'remembering.' This is equivalent to the Arabic, *zikr,* the continual remembrance of God.

Khwaja Baha' ad-Din Naqshband tells us that the purpose of *zikr* is that "the heart be always aware of *al-Haqq*"—God, the Truth—and that the practice of *zikr* banishes our natural tendency to inattentiveness.[33] Likewise, Khwaja 'Ubaidallah al-Ahrar says that the real meaning of *zikr* is the achievement of an "inward awareness of God," and the practice of *zikr* is only to help us "attain this consciousness."[34]

Our 'remembering' of God is usually expressed and accomplished through the use of a *wazifa,* a sacred word or formula, repeated until it is seated in consciousness. This is the *practice* of *zikr.*

In the first principle, *hosh dar dam, Allah* is conceived as the breath itself, the subtle essence pervading and penetrating all things. In this fifth principle, *'Allah'* is the sacred word repeatedly entered into consciousness. The word becomes an object of meditation, a *wazifa,* placed on the breath . . . *Allah, Allah, Allah, Allah.*[35]

The repetition can be silent or vocal, *zikr khafi* or *zikr jahri.* But whether on the tongue or in the mind, the goal is to keep a connection to the heart, transforming the *zikr* of the tongue or mind into the *zikr* of the heart. As J.G. Bennett so aptly put it, "what we feel we should say and what we say we should feel."[36]

In this step of the eight-fold process, you are adding a more specific object of meditation to help you hold your focus, because meditation is really the replacement of many unintentional thoughts with one particular thought. You do not turn the mind off; you just occupy it differently.

When you really watch your thoughts, you see that you are not actually thinking one thought at a time. The mouth may be a serial instrument, but the mind is not. You can only say one word at a time, but the mind contains a myriad of concurrent thoughts, one layered upon another, even when it seems that one particular thought is occupying you.

The mind is really a flow-phenomenon, and one way of dealing with it is to add a sacred 'agent' or 'emulsifier' to it, like dye coloring water.

The choice of 'agent' is important. Our minds are occupied with all kinds of things, not necessarily helpful or meritorious. When we choose to occupy it, we must choose carefully.

When I was a young man, I had the privilege of sitting at the feet of Khenpo Tsultrim Gyamtso, a Tibetan Buddhist meditation master of the Kagyu tradition. He was generally called 'Khenpo Rinpoche,' after his learned title. It was an acknowledgment of his learning and accomplishment, something like calling him, 'The Doctor.' He was known as a great scholar of *madhyamika,* the non-dual philosophy of Buddhism, and for being a great practitioner, often meditating in mountain caves.

I remember sitting directly in front of him. He was one of those Tibetan lamas who laughed a lot, a deep, hearty laugh, while still maintaining a penetrating look in his eyes. He seemed to find everything funny, especially the things he said himself! At various points in his talk, he would stop and sing a *doha*, or enlightenment song, some of which he made up in the course of his talk.

What I remember most, however, is Khenpo Rinpoche looking at us and saying very clearly—"All of spirituality is keeping better company . . . Better friends, better surroundings, better thoughts."[37]

That's it.

Now ask yourself what you care about, what one thought you would choose to unite and color the myriad thoughts flowing in your mind. That is what you want to remember in *zikr!* What connects and unites is remembrance, as Shah Kalim Allah Jahanabadi writes in his *Kashkul-i Kalimi* . . .

> Meditation is remembrance as opposed to forgetfulness. So whatever makes you remember and stay connected with your object (God) counts as meditation and constitutes an act of worship *('ibadat)*, regardless of whether the means of meditation be a name, ritual or action performed with the body or in the body or in any other way. Likewise, whatever makes you forget and neglect your object (God) is misguided and vain, regardless of whether the means of forgetting be a name, person, thing or anything else. For Sufis, everything said, everything done and everything felt can be meditation, on condition that it leads them to remember God and stay awake and aware. Anything which does not promote remembering is forgetfulness and should be shunned, as conveyed in this couplet:
>
> If I am with you, my daily work is prayer
> And without you, my prayer is merely work.[38]

6. *Baz Gasht* – 'Returning!'

The sixth principle is *baz gasht*, 'coming back' or 'returning.' *Baz* is also the word for 'falcon' in Arabic and Farsi. In these cultures where falconry was common, you can easily see how the falcon going out in search of prey and returning to the master's gloved hand might be associated and brought together in the word, *'baz.'*

Now, you might ask, 'How is *returning* different from the third principle, *journey homeward?'* The answer is: it is the difference between finding the path and falling away from it.

However hard we try to hold the internal center we have found *(khilvat dar anjuman),* placing God in the forefront of our awareness *(yad kard),* a wind eventually blows so hard that we are knocked off course, or so gently that we are distracted from the journey homeward *(safar dar vatan)* and it becomes necessary to return *(baz gasht).*

Getting lost is simply part of the path, part of the process of journeying homeward. It teaches us humility, compassion for others, and how to find our way back. It also teaches us about where we do not want to find ourselves again.[39]

It is a principle that applies to the meditative process as well. We drift away and need to come back.

Imagine you are meditating . . . *meditating, meditating, meditating* . . . Then, 'Oh, I forgot to take the laundry out of the dryer,' or you drift off into a memory of something that happened years ago. You are unaware of how long you have been caught up in these thoughts—five minutes, ten minutes—when suddenly, 'Oh, where was I?' Then you return to the breath, remembering *'Allah.'*

Baz gasht means, 'Your attention has drifted—come back!'

This is a basic feature of meditation—*impermanence.* We cannot hold a singular focus permanently. Thus, Khwaja 'Abd al-Khaliq Ghujdawani recommends that we intersperse our *zikr* with the words attributed to the Prophet—*Ilahi-anta maqsudi wa-ridhaka matlubi*, 'My God, you are my goal, and your pleasure my desire.'[40]

7. *Nigah Dasht* – 'Watchfulness!'

Coming back, *baz gasht,* it is now clear to the traveler just how easy it is to get lost or blown off course in life. Thus, some other quality is required to keep us on the right path; in this case, the seventh principle, *nigah dasht,* 'watchfulness' or 'attentiveness.'

But what is it that will keep us attentive and vigilant as we journey homeward? It is not enough to say, 'I need to be more attentive!' First, we need to know *why* we have to be more attentive; we need a compelling reason for it.

Fuel is required to power all of our endeavors. If we want to make a great fire, we need wood to burn and a spark to light it. Look at what it takes to put a ship into Space—massive fuel tanks and a powerful explosion of energy to overcome the gravitational pull of the Earth. Likewise, if we want to achieve escape velocity from the gravity-pull of our unhealthy habits and behaviors, we need a massive amount of energy to power the change, more than what is already keeping those habits in place.

Often, the most immediate and compelling reason is some sort of dissatisfaction. Dissatisfaction can be a powerful tool of transformation if harnessed to that end. Wanting some other kind of life, we are often ready to do whatever is necessary to reach that goal. In that case, we hold on to the dissatisfaction, using the chain of our own bondage to pull us toward the freedom we desire.

Perhaps less immediately compelling, but deeper and more important, is a vision of our own wholeness and nobility. When this is combined with our dissatisfaction, we often find the winning combination to fuel our change and hold our ground in the struggle for it. While dissatisfaction can fuel our initial escape velocity, breaking us out of a pattern, a strong connection to a vision can actually create more stability of purpose in us. As the vision acquires spiritual mass over time, its own gravitational forces grow, anchoring us to our purpose and keeping us grounded.

My *murshid* used to encourage us to actually live that vision, saying, "Try to spend even fifteen minutes each day living that reality."[41] Likewise, Shaykh Muhammad Hisham Kabbani, who we once visited, has written: "It is acknowledged in the Naqshbandi Order that for a seeker to safeguard his heart from bad inclinations for fifteen minutes is a great achievement. For this he would be considered a real Sufi."[42]

In *zikr*, 'watchfulness,' or *nigah dasht,* is being aware of what distracts you and 'doubling-down' on your commitment to the goal.[43] That we get distracted may be inevitable, but how frequently we are distracted is not.

The masters of the tradition tell us that it is not enough to say, *'Allah, Allah, Allah, Allah,'* merely with the tongue. *Allah* must be fixed in our hearts, too. *Allah* has to mean something; it has to be compelling enough for me to want to hold on to it.

The questions are: What does it mean to me? And why am I doing this?

When we forget the reasons, we lose focus and drift off. The reasons need to be present enough to help me hold on and do the practice in a committed way.

Many years ago, a close friend of mine, a Tibetan Buddhist monk, was doing his *ngondro*—a particular tantric liturgy performed each day, accompanied by visualizations, and requiring as many as 100,000 prostrations, while holding a close focus. It might take a person a year or even years to finish their *ngondro* properly. Well, my friend was doing his *ngondro* in India under the guidance of Boker Rinpoche, a disciple of the great Kalu Rinpoche, and came to see Boker Rinpoche, who inquired, "How many prostrations have you done?"

He reported confidently, "I'm up to 30,000!"

Then Boker Rinpoche asked, "How many good ones?" That is to say, 'For how many were you present?'

My friend started over.[44]

We ask the same question in *zikr*—'For how many were you present? . . . Ninety-nine or eleven?' We usually aspire to *at least* a round of ninety-nine on the *tesbiḥ;* but how many rounds of ninety-nine do you have to do to actually be present for ninety-nine? Nine rounds? Think about that the next time you sit down to do your *zikr.*

Thus, the masters urge us to be "vigilant" in controlling our attention, safeguarding the heart from allowing anything other than God to enter it.[45]

On retreat, doing more intensive *khalwah* (retreat) practices, I would try to hold this ideal of 'attentiveness' firmly. I would get through a single round of ninety-nine repetitions and say to myself, "How many was I really present for?" And with all the integrity I could muster, I would then add another ninety-nine if I thought it necessary. And when I had finished those ninety-nine, I would ask again, "And how many was I really present for?" Then I might do ninety-nine more, just hoping in the end that I would have a total of ninety-nine sincerely devoted remembrances as I had actually intended when I began!

Nigah dasht is the will and desire to hold firm in that commitment.

8. Yad Dasht – 'Remembrance!'

Finally, we come to the eighth principle, *yad dasht,* 'remembrance.'

The fifth principle is *yad kard,* 'remembering,' or *zikr.* And now we have *yad dasht,* 'remembrance.'

What is the difference between 'remembering' and 'remembrance'?

Consider for a moment the two ways in which we use the word 'meditation.' Meditation is both the activity of meditating and also the state it facilitates. Likewise, *yad kard* is the activity of *zikr,* actively remembering God . . . *Allah, Allah, Allah, Allah.*[46] While *yad dasht* is actually being *in* remembrance. It is no longer a conscious activity, but a state of consciousness, a reality in the present moment of the remember-er *(zakir).* That experiential reality, being 'in remembrance,' is considered a 'taste' *(zawq)* of the divine presence, the repeated experience of which, anchors that presence in the heart.[47] According to the masters, it is the "experience of divine contemplation, achieved through the action of objective Love,"[48] casting away three of the four different kinds of thought—wicked thoughts, egotistical thoughts, and angelic thoughts—and grounding one in the experience of "truthful thoughts," an experience of the 'unity of all being,' *waḥdat al-wujud.*[49]

The Inward Journey

Now, if we look at these eight principles as steps in a meditative process, we can see how each clearly represents a stage of an inward journey.

Imagine that I am in seated meditation and bring my awareness to my breath—*hosh dar dam*—finding a relationship with the most basic process of our lives, connecting me with the subtle essence that connects all being.

Now I make it rhythmic—*nazar bar qadam*—watching 'the steps' of the breaths, one following the other . . . one, two, three, four.

Watching these steps, I begin the inward journey—*safar dar vatan*—following the slow, deep progression of my breath.

My senses begin to withdraw and I move further and further inward, eventually achieving a peaceful, centered place—*khilvat dar anjuman*.

In this peaceful, centered place, we remember *'Allah'*—*yad kard*—introducing this object of meditation into our consciousness, again and again . . . *'Allah, Allah, Allah, Allah.'*

Before I know it, I realize suddenly that I have been gone on a tangent, lost in other thoughts, and I return—*baz gasht*—to the object of my meditation, *'Allah.'*

Now, fearing the loss of all my progress, I strengthen my resolve and commitment to holding my focus—*nigah dasht*.

Holding that focus, a transition is made from conscious activity to a state of consciousness—*yad dasht*—wherein remembering becomes remembrance.

These are the *kalimat-i qudsiyya*, the 'sacred words' of the Khwajaghan, and our inheritance from them.[50] They describe and direct us on the greater path of Sufism, and at the same time, serve as simple guidelines for a meditative practice of *zikr*, 'remembrance.'

For those who desire it, there is plenty of 'fancy Sufism' out there, enough esoterica and intellectual brilliance to occupy them for a lifetime. But that, in and of itself, is not Sufism. Sufism is the practice and experience of *tasawwuf*, 'purification.' It is the work of being a Sufi, seeking a relationship of intimacy with God.

Every great teacher I have known—though brilliant each in their own way, and often deeply learned in esoteric teaching—has done the basic work of Sufism, dedicating themselves to deepening in relationship to simple and effective practices. The most elegant and beautiful theory must fall silent in awe and humility before the difficult essentials of real life and practice.

Transformation comes from experience, not books or talks about experience; not even this one. Sometimes you will hear someone disparage 'the basics of practice,' saying, 'That's not the deep stuff.' The truth is, there is no *'deep stuff.'* You are just deep, or you are not, whether in reading the most elevated mystical text, or in the simplicity of bowing your head before the ultimate. Deep is what you bring, not what you get.

Thus, we come back to the anthem of the Sufis, the chant of the dervishes in the cemetery . . .

Hosh dar dam!
Nazar bar qadam!
Safar dar vatan!
Khilvat dar anjuman!

‘eshq

The Three Deaths of Love

An Introduction to the Sufi Path of Love *

Long ago, in a forgotten sultanate of the East, there was a group of young men who used to hang out in the *suq*, in the open market near the gates of the sultan's palace. These were young men who hadn't yet found their way—some of them not even sure that they wanted to find *'a way'*—so they hung out in the market, gambling and joking around, and only when necessary, getting an odd job to earn enough to buy a little food or gamble with again at night.

One day, as they were sitting near the gates of the palace, a little bored with the usual fare, and with each other, one of them who was the most bored, noticed a sedan chair—the kind used for carrying the women of the court—approaching the gates. So he got up to see if he could get a better look. Then he saw a sight such as he had never seen before: a young woman . . . but not like the young women he knew, not like the ordinary girls of the market. She seemed to him a rare pearl, smooth and radiant, almost not of this world, at least not of the squalid world he knew. Obviously, it was the princess.

* An edited version of a talk originally given in Portland, Oregon on July 9th, 2016 at Lewis and Clark College for the Season of the Rose, the annual summer school of the Inayati Order, and later in New Lebanon, New York, May 12-13th, 2017, at the Abode of the Message, during "Rasa Shastra: Exploring Love, Intimacy, Sex, and Relationships in Sufism" with Deepa Gulrukh Patel.

She stepped down from the sedan with the greatest elegance and quickly entered the gate; but not before the young man had gotten a good look at her beautiful countenance and gentle form. Utterly captivated, he was chained to the spot on which he was standing; staring at the closed gate, mouth agape, still seeing the image of the beautiful princess in his mind, he was suddenly *and rudely* awakened from his reverie by a slap on the back and the raucous laughter of his friends!

Realizing they were laughing at him, he quickly recovered and said coarsely, "What I wouldn't give for two hours alone with *her!"*

His friends laughed again, but this time with him; for that was how they thought of young women. And the truth was, he wasn't much different. But even as they walked away laughing, arm-in-arm, he found himself looking back over his shoulder.

That night, he lay awake thinking of her. And yes, in the way young men usually do; but there was also something else, something he couldn't quite put his finger on. So the next day, instead of going to hang out with his friends as he had always done, he made a different choice, and went back to the gates of the palace, alone. He hoped once again to catch a glimpse of the beautiful princess. He waited all day, but was disappointed; she didn't come. But so strong was his desire to see her that he returned again the next day.

Day after day passed in this way, and he occasionally thought of other things he might be doing, the things he used to do with his friends; but they just didn't seem to have the same allure anymore. He couldn't conceive of hanging out with his friends and gambling now if it meant missing the opportunity of seeing the princess again. The old pleasures now paled before the possibility of encountering her beauty. Over time, even food began to lose its flavor for him, and he became somewhat melancholy. He wondered what was wrong with him. *Maybe,* he thought, *I should try to rid myself of her image?*

So, as he had done in the past, he went out with his friends again, drinking and gambling—though the Qur'an wisely warns about the danger of these activities. Clearly, he was hoping to quench his desires with them. He even pursued other young women, far easier to catch than the elusive princess. But nothing worked. Nothing sated his desire for her.

Thus, once more, he took himself back to the gate, and each day waited near the entrance, hoping to catch a glimpse of the rare and beautiful princess. He only wanted to see her again and proclaim his love. He was a simple young man, after all, and thoughtless of the almost insurmountable obstacles involved in loving a princess.

Then, after weeks of waiting—what seemed an eternity—he caught sight of the same sedan chair coming toward the gate. She must have come out while he was sleeping or trying to lose himself in other pursuits. But here she was again, finally!

Overwhelmed by his great passion, he did the unthinkable, or at least something very unwise . . . Before the guards could stop him, he leapt toward the sedan, just as the princess was stepping out!

Throwing himself at her feet, he kissed the hem of her dress, saying—"My princess, my love, when can we be together?!"

The princess, of course, was taken aback. But, maintaining her royal cool, she took one look at the brash young man, dressed in rags, and said with polite disdain, "In the *cemetery.*" Meaning, of course, 'Not in this lifetime, buddy!' She then pulled away and entered the gate as the guards grabbed the young man and threw him aside, roughly.

But the young man was ecstatic! You see, for him, there was only his love and the object of his love. He thought that all he had to do was proclaim it! He could not even conceive that she might not share it. He assumed, like many young men, that the depth of his feelings implied her own. So, poor, simple young man that he was—with no experience of the subtleties of the educated—he took her seriously and headed straight for the cemetery.

"Yes!" He said to himself, "No one will see us there! We can be alone! The dead have no eyes! . . . My beloved is smart as well as beautiful!"

Reaching the outskirts of the city, he entered the cemetery and began to look around for the best place for their 'encounter,' which is to say, the most romantic and advantageous spot in the cemetery for making love! But no sooner did he find one spot than he gave it up in favor of another. Nothing seemed quite good enough, until finally, by every measure he could conceive, he found the most ideal spot and sat down to wait for her.

After a number of hours, he said to himself—"I suppose it's not so easy for a princess to get away from the palace. The sultan probably watches her like a hawk. And didn't I have to wait weeks to see her again at the gate? It may be that I'll have to wait just as long here. But it'll be worth it! Here at least we can be together, alone!"

So he waited, imagining the beautiful face of his beloved and their reunion.

As the days passed, he got by doing a little begging, and sometimes spent his time walking around the cemetery, looking at the gravestones. He didn't dare leave the cemetery, as he had already learned his lesson at the gate.

Looking at the markers now, he saw that some people had lived to be very old, while others had died young. Some, from the look of their stones, were obviously rich, while others poor. Some—he overheard people saying—had perished in accidents, while others had merely succumbed to old age. Naturally, he started to ponder these matters, wondering what it was all about. And sometimes these thoughts joined with thoughts of his beloved and her beauty, to which he always returned, never forgetting why he was there in the first place.

Weeks and months passed. People came to the cemetery

to bury their loved ones, to visit their graves, and he saw them crying, and heard them say things like, "She was so pretty when she was young," or "He was such a handsome man," and he began to think about these comments.

One day, he asked himself—"What is it I've fallen in love with in the princess? Is it her physical beauty? That is wonderful, certainly, but it will change. She will get old and her beauty will fade; and finally, she'll end up here . . . just bones. But many people come and bury their loved ones here who are no longer beautiful, and yet, their love seems to remain. Will I continue to love the princess when she is no longer beautiful?"

Thus, he began to think about the meaning of beauty and the nature of love, and eventually, he realized that beauty comes in many forms, not all of them physical. He wondered aloud, "Is there a beauty that does not change, that one may love forever? Indeed, what is the source of beauty and love?

"I suppose," he said, "it must be God. . . . God must be the source of beauty and love. Indeed, God must be more beautiful than anything on earth." But try as he might, he could not imagine what that beauty might be like, or really of anything more beautiful than his princess.

In some ways, hers was the face of God for him. But he knew from the preachers that God does not have a face such as we have, and must somehow be more beautiful than his princess, who was only one of God's creations. So he began to summon all the images of beauty he had ever known or could conceive—delicate jasmine, great cypresses, sparkling waters, majestic mountains, and vast blue skies. Even the weathered stones of the cemetery and the rust on the gates had a kind of beauty of their own, he thought.

More and more images of beauty passed before his mind's eye now, and he began to bring them together—*the princess and the weathered stones of the cemetery implanted in the earth, from which grew the delicate jasmine and the tall cypresses which touched the sky, which held his thoughts, where dwelt the image of his beloved*—until all the things he could conceive created a vision of the totality of being, a beautiful unity of all being, to which he and everything belonged, and suddenly, suddenly, he passed out in utter bliss!

Now, for a long time, people had noticed that this young man was always in the cemetery. At first, they thought he must be doing penance, and so they offered him a little food. But later, when they saw he never left the cemetery, and seemed more and more absorbed in his meditation, they thought, *This must be a holy man, a saint!* So they began to bring him food on a regular basis, and even to ask him for advice and blessings.

For all the young man knew, he was just waiting for the princess and puzzling over a question. But as the months and years passed, his beard grew long, and spending so much time in the cemetery, he had actually become a thoughtful person. So now when someone asked his advice, he would tell them what he thought, or say, "I'll think about it; come back later and we'll talk." And when people asked him for blessings, and he looked at their sorrow and their needs, touching his own pain and longing for the absent princess, he would simply speak the wish of that aching heart, "May there be help for you." And these blessings seemed to work.

In the meantime, the princess did what princesses do; she married a prince in a marriage of diplomacy. Fortunately for her, it was a happy marriage; she grew to love the prince, and he was good to her. There was just one problem. She didn't become pregnant, or when she did, she didn't carry to term. And this was the great pain of her life. She tried every doctor, near and far, every herb from every local healer, even the expensive and useless charms offered by all the local charlatans. Money was no object, but nothing worked. Finally, one of her servants, unable to bear the sadness of her mistress any longer, said to her—"My lady, I know it is not my place to suggest anything; but when the people of this city need help, they go to the holy man in the cemetery for a blessing. Perhaps you could visit him, too, and ask his blessing for a child?"

Concealing her last hope under the garments of her maid, the princess went disguised to the cemetery in the dark of night to seek the saint's blessing.

Seeing the holy man seated in meditation in a quiet corner of the cemetery, his back against a headstone, she approached and spoke to him, saying, *"Mawla,"* master.

Hearing her voice, the saint of the cemetery looked up from his meditation—and though many years had passed—he recognized her immediately and said in a gentle, quiet voice—"My princess, you have kept your promise."

Taken aback, the princess disguised in the clothes of her maid said, "How could you possibly know who I am?!"

"Because," he replied, "I was the young man at the gate, the one you said you would meet 'in the cemetery.' . . . And all these many years, I have kept your image before me. And I want to thank you. It was your beauty and your guidance that sent me here, where I have come to know many great things, and indeed, where I have found the source of beauty and the source of my love.

"But, princess, no one comes to me in joy. They all come in sorrow. Tell me then, what is your sorrow?"

The princess then began to cry and unburden herself to the saint, telling him of her sorrow, and asking a blessing that she might become pregnant and deliver a child in safety.

The saint of the cemetery sighed. He loved her still.

"If there is any merit in anything I have done in this life," he said, sadness filling his throat, "I would want that merit to be transformed into a child for you."

And this is how he blessed her.

He then turned away from her to gaze upon his love.

Sometime later, people noticed that he was deeper in

meditation than usual and tried not to disturb him. But when a few days had passed, and still he didn't come out of his meditation, and the food that had been laid before him remained untouched, they became concerned. Finally, someone came close and found that he was no longer breathing. He had died in the cemetery, gazing at the source of beauty.

But his final blessing had worked; the princess became pregnant, and the pregnancy held. At first, she was cautiously optimistic; but as time went by, she could feel the health of the child in her, and when the time was ripe, she delivered the baby safely.

When the baby was old enough to take out of the palace, she announced to her maid that she wished to take the boy for a blessing from the saint of the cemetery. But her maid looked distressed and said—"Oh my lady, has no one told you? . . . The saint of the cemetery died in his meditation not long after you visited him."

Hearing this, the princess mourned him sincerely, and ordered a great tomb erected in the place where the saint had died in his meditation.

Years later, however, when her son was old enough to understand, she brought him to the tomb of the saint of the cemetery, and there told him the story of the love that had made his birth possible.[1]

Knowledge, Love, and Passionate Love

Sufism is a tradition whose stories, poetry, and teachings celebrate divine love, and whose practices are intended to cultivate an experience of it.

There are two basic words which Sufis use when talking about love—*mahabba* and *'ishq* or *'eshq*.

Mahabba is 'loving-kindness,' the love we feel for our friends, our families, and our partners. It is love, pure and simple, a love which arises out of *ma'rifah,* or gnosis. Gnosis is experiential knowledge, something you know because you have 'tasted' it, or 'touched' it. You have had an experience of it; and even if you cannot articulate or describe it fully, the knowledge is simply *there*, present in your bones.

In Sufism, we are taught that love is greater than knowledge, and yet grows out of the ground of a knowledge born of experience.[2] What does that mean? You do not feel love for a person until you have had an experience of them, until you have 'tasted' their presence in some way. This 'tasting' is called *zawq*. Something about the person awakens or stimulates a resonance of love in you, a feeling of *mahabba.*

But still greater than *mahabba,* according to Sufis, is *'eshq.*[3] *'Eshq* is passionate love, fiery love. *'Eshq* is derived from the word, *'ashaqah,* which is a type of vine that winds itself tightly around a tree, almost strangling it, like bittersweet.[4] It has a beautiful flower, but so tight and passionate is its hold on the tree that it can squeeze the life out of it, just as passionate love, in the right circumstances, can squeeze the life from the ego, leaving only love in its place.

Mahabba is baseline love. *'Eshq* is love that rises above the baseline. The baseline love of *mahabba* is necessary; it is like an ember that can always be blown upon and burst into flame again. When it is in flame, it is *'eshq*.

Now, if you are in a relationship long enough, the *'eshq* of the first flush of falling in love will eventually die down to the baseline *mahabba.* It is a good thing; it is the steady love of a long-term relationship. But it is also so steady that it can sometimes be forgotten, like white noise; after a little while, sometimes you cannot hear it anymore. It is at this point that we sometimes ask ourselves, 'Am I still in love?' It is so steady and quiet that you can even begin to wonder whether it still exists . . . that is, until something happens that makes you afraid. Maybe your beloved gets sick, or is in danger, or the relationship is in trouble, God forbid; then, just watch as the feelings burst into flame again!

And this is not only applicable to romantic relationships; the same thing can happen with a parent, a child, a friend, or even a stranger in the right circumstances; for *mahabba* is basic love and affection, and *'eshq* the passionate intensity that arises to fuel or protect it.

In some cases, the *'eshq* is so intense that it can burn everything around it. It is the love about which the Song of Songs says . . .

many waters
cannot quench love
nor can floods drown it

for love is as strong as death
passion as cruel as the grave

its flashes
are flashes of fire
the very flame of god[5]

This is not the sentimental love of dewy-eyed romantics. It is burning in the fires of love. This is a lover who knows the experience of *'ashaqah,* the experience of being strangled by the intensity of a painful love. It is the love that flames up and transforms a person, transforms them because its intensity has burned them to ashes. As Jalal ad-Din Rumi writes . . .

Love is the flame
which when it blazes up,
burns away everything
except the beloved.[6]

This is the model of love in Sufism.

The question is—Who is the object of that love? God or a human being?

In the poetry of Hafez, it is rarely clear whether he is talking about a human or a divine beloved. Sometimes he seems to be in love with a young man, sometimes a young woman, and sometimes it is clearly God. It is all in the play of the poetry, and it is difficult to distinguish a single, distinct object of love.

And sometimes it is abundantly clear . . .

To give up wine, and human beauty? And to give up love?
No, I won't do it.
A hundred times I said I would; what was I thinking of?
No, I won't do it.

To say that paradise, its houris, and its shade are more
To me than the dusty street before my lover's door?
No, I won't do it.[7]

In these stanzas, we see Hafez dealing with those who are telling him that he must transcend human love in favor of a more refined, divine love. These are Sufis who say that human love is only *'eshq-i majazi,* 'apparent love,' while love of God is *'eshq-i haqiqi,* 'real love.' But Hafez and many other Sufis suggest that this is a distinction without a difference, that the only way to love God is through loving the world and other human beings, for these are the manifestations of that divinity. How else can I touch God except through my beloved, my friend, and lover? And is that not the best way to worship, by acknowledging the sacredness of all creation?

Ultimately, the distinction between 'human' or 'divine' love falls apart in the non-dual 'unity of all being'—*waḥdat al-wujud*—where everything is God; thus, there is never any love that is not ultimately offered to God.

The Death of the World

In the teachings of the younger brother of Imam Abu Hamid Ghazzali, Shaykh Ahmad Ghazzali (ca. 1061-1126), who is considered the founder of the Sufi 'school of love' *(mazhab-i 'eshq),* we find a simple description of how a person is spiritually transformed through love; for he writes, in the fourth chapter of his *Sovaneh,* that the experience of love in its depths is actually an experience of a succession of spiritual deaths.[8]

The first death, he says, is the death of the world, or worldly expectations.[9] Much of our lives are driven by these expectations, and it is a mark of the depth of love to be able to release them in favor of the love relationship.

From one perspective, this happens naturally in the early intoxication of love, as described in a line of poetry in Anthony Minghella's *The English Patient* . . .

Betrayals in war
are childlike
compared with our betrayals
during peace.

New lovers
are nervous and tender
but smash everything,
for the heart is an organ of fire.[10]

How many of us know this experience of 'smashing everything' when falling in love? Colliding with another person at an inopportune moment in time, creating chaos in the world around us, the world forgotten in the whirlwind of discovery in which we are then enveloped?

When I was young, I fell in love with a young woman who I would later marry. I fell in love with her in the same year my grandmother was dying. My grandmother had raised me and I adored her; but she was all but forgotten in that first mystical spring of falling in love, and I missed the opportunity of spending more of those last precious months with her. I still feel guilty about it; but there was nothing I could do; I was lost in the wonder of an experience over which I had little control. Still later, in falling in love again, I would smash more things I never intended, creating even deeper regrets; for, as the poem says, "the heart is an organ of fire."

But there is also a more important, more conscious process in which we deny the world as we make decisions for love. New lovers may easily forget the world, forget their friends, and responsibilities; but what happens when the world pushes back and places obstacles and difficulties in the lover's path?

The young woman I married was from a good middle-class Christian family, got good grades in school, and for the most part, followed her family's expectations. But those expectations did not include marrying a boy from the other side of the tracks. I was from a poor, working-class Mexican-American family (and Jewish, too!), and on the surface, not a very good prospect. Some of her family believed I would drag her down. So they intervened and actively tried to convince her not to marry me. But, God bless her, she saw something in me, believed in me, and stood up to them. It was more than rebellion; it was character, and it meant the world to me that she pushed back against the expectations of her family.

But often, the stakes are much higher. Not so long ago, and still in some places around the world, the societal pressures and social sanctions for falling in love with someone of the same sex, another race or religion, or anyone really of whom the general culture does not approve, could mean real losses. It might mean that you could not get a job, or buy a home in a certain neighborhood, or worse, that you might be arrested, imprisoned, beaten, or even killed. To choose love over fear in such situations is a profound act of bravery—it is the death of the world.

In the medieval period, we get the first great stories in the West of heroes and heroines who choose love over worldly censure. They are mostly stories of illicit love, because illicit love was then considered *'true love.'* Not illicit sex, but illicit love. Love outside the boundaries of marriage and societal expectations.

Why was this considered true love?

Because there were no rewards.

Marriage at the time was mostly a social contract, a marriage of convenience meant to achieve certain societal ends. To fall in love with someone outside of those expectations was a recipe for pain and unhappiness. You were not going to get to have one another, and if you did in any way, the consequences were so harsh that happiness was hardly possible—loss of family, friends, possessions, and your place in society. Thus, anyone who chose such a love was thought to be truly in love, because there was no advantage.

The classic story of this kind of love is that of Tristan and Isolde. Though there are various tellings of the story, the most profound and beautiful is that of Gottfried Von Strassburg, who really, for the first time in the western world, articulates a true philosophy of love.

Tristan was a knight of the Arthurian world attached to his uncle, King Mark of Cornwall. He was not only a great warrior, but also a handsome and gifted poet. Women loved him, men loved him, and his uncle the king loved him most, making him his heir. But some of the king's counselors were also jealous of Tristan, and gave the king no peace, begging him to take a wife who would give him a true son and heir. Finally, their plotting reached a head and Tristan said to his uncle, "Let's be done with this uncle; I have no need to be your heir. Let me make a match for you with Princess Isolde of Ireland, of whom we have spoken. She is a woman of the greatest beauty and virtue, with whom you could not fail to be happy."

His uncle agreed and Tristan set off for Ireland.

There was just one problem: *Isolde hated Tristan.* She hated him because he had killed her uncle, Morold, in single combat. Thus, to her, the name *Tristan* was anathema.

For this reason, Tristan came to Ireland disguised as a wandering minstrel called Tantris. Winning the favor of the court of the king, charming everyone, Tristan (as Tantris) finally says: "You know, there is a wonderful match for your daughter, Isolde. King Mark of my own country—Cornwall—is a good man and a truly honorable king. He'll be a good husband for her and will treat her well. And in this way, there will be peace between Cornwall and Ireland, and your grandchildren will unite the two kingdoms!"

The king was convinced and Tristan negotiated the terms of the deal for his uncle, King Mark; for this is what it was in those days, a 'transaction' between two royal families. And yet, even as he executed this plan, Tristan was aware that at some point, he was going to have to tell Isolde the truth . . . and she was not going to be happy.

The contract signed, Tristan and Isolde (with her maidservant, Brangane) boarded a ship bound for Cornwall.

Now Isolde's mother was a wise woman and a witch. And because her daughter was being married in a political marriage, as she herself had been, she was worried. Happiness in such marriages is far from certain. So she decided to mix a love potion in a little bottle of wine, instructing the maidservant, Brangane, to serve it to Isolde and King Mark on their wedding night. They will drink together and fall in love, and thus their marriage will be a true one.

Meanwhile, on board the ship, Isolde, who has now discovered Tristan's true identity—*T-a-n-t-r-i-s* is *T-r-i-s-t-a-n*—is furious! But she is also in a bind, as Tristan well knows. After all, she is to be married to his uncle, and he is his uncle's favorite nephew. They are going to have to work it out.

Finally, she says to Tristan, "How can I be in a good marriage if I can't get along with the most beloved friend and servant of my husband?" So they agree to make peace and talk things out.

Tristan tells her: "Look, I am a knight. Your uncle and I were on opposing sides of a war. He was a great warrior, but I was the lucky one that day and prevailed. I'm truly sorry."

Isolde accepts his apology, and says: "Well, I liked you when I thought you were the wandering minstrel, Tantris. So maybe we can be friends."

They decide to bury the hatchet, saying, "We'll have a meal and toast our friendship over a glass of wine."

They call for Brangane, but she is nowhere to be found. So a servant goes searching through their belongings for some wine and discovers a beautiful little bottle in one of Isolde's chests. It seems perfect for the occasion.

Tristan pours the wine; they toast and drink.

Suddenly, each is unexpectedly flooded with emotion. It is as if the scales have fallen from their eyes and they now see one another in a new light! The love and passion is so palpable between them that they almost cannot refrain from touching one another, and both are immediately panic-stricken and terrified! Neither thinks, *Oh, this is beautiful!* It is awful and they know it. It is awful because he loves his uncle and she is his uncle's promised bride. Both know that this love means suffering and betraying the trust of their families and friends.

They immediately flee to opposite ends of the ship. But a strange compulsion keeps drawing them back together. They can't be too close, nor too far from one another. They pass and brush one another in corridors and unexpectedly enter the same room, until finally, it is too much, and Tristan takes Isolde in his arms and kisses her. They pull apart again and agree that they must not give in to this temptation. But being apart proves too difficult and they soon begin to arrange meetings in secret, avoiding Brangane whenever possible. They feel worse and worse, even as they find greater and greater satisfaction with one another.

When Brangane is around, they pretend to fight and hate one another as before. But Brangane is not blind; something doesn't seem right to her. She catches looks out of the corner of her eye and feels the sudden shifts in the air when she enters a room. Finally, she catches a look that is undeniable, and in horror, remembers the potion! She runs to the chest where it was hidden and finds it gone! Then, coming upon the empty bottle in the galley, confronts Tristan, holding the empty bottle and saying, *"You have drunk your death!"*

Tristan, knowing that they have finally been discovered, responds in resolute sorrow—"If by my 'death,' you mean the pain of this love I now feel, well that is my life. If by my 'death' you mean that I will certainly be killed for loving this woman I should not, I accept that. But if by my death you mean that I will certainly suffer eternal torment in the fires of hell . . . *well, then I accept that, too!*"[11]

That is, as Hazrat Inayat Khan puts it, accepting "the bowl of poison from the hands of love as nectar."[12] For Tristan, it means accepting the pain and heavy punishments that will come with it, because he is simply in the throes of love and cannot be out of it.

And yet, people make the opposite choice all the time, refusing the "bowl of poison." There are people who are really in love that choose to give in to societal pressures, or who make choices that are determined by their fears. The love may remain, despite their choices, but the relationship often ends, or is disrupted. It is a mark of the deepening of love in relationship if you can transcend those fears, or overcome the pressures which would disrupt it. Thus, the obstacle becomes the threshold of a deeper relationship.

In this case, Tristan will not be without Isolde. He is willing to give up the world for her, and even heaven, the ultimate reward, for now love has become his ultimate reward, and worth suffering the ultimate punishment in hell.

That is the death of the world, as Ahmad Ghazzali conceives it. And yet, it is only the first of three deaths into love.

The Death of the Self

The second death he describes is the death of the self.

Of course, there is an aspect of this in the death of the world, too, as we have seen. If for love I give up my worldly prospects or my reputation, it is certainly a death for the self, a yielding of ego for love.

It was not until I was an adult that I really came to appreciate the fact that my parents were an interracial couple in the 1960s. My father, who worked for the railroad, was Anglo, and my mother, a factory worker, was Mexican. My father's mother actually wore black to their wedding, mourning the fact that her son was marrying a Mexican woman! It only occurred to me later that this was an act of courage on my father's part, and that he had a quality of character for which I had not credited him when I was growing up.

So there is a death of the self, a noble yielding of self, in the willingness to suffer worldly censure or consequences for love; but this is not the specific death of which Ahmad Ghazzali is concerned in this instance.[13]

The lover who endures difficulties for the sake of the beloved is acting nobly, but their actions are still basically driven by their own desire "to have and to hold" the beloved.[14] A further degree of selflessness comes when one is faced with the question—*Can I give up my own desires or fears for the needs and desires of my beloved?*

An aspect of love's depth is the ability to weigh the desires and concerns of one's beloved above one's own. That is to say, love both *allows us* and *gives us* the opportunity to forget ourselves and move beyond selfish love. In love, we have the opportunity to want only 'the good' of the other, or at least, to want it enough to yield our own desires or fears and give without expectation of return.

Imagine you married young and struggled for many years. You live on little, and it takes you and your partner a long time to dig yourselves out of debt—debt from student loans, medical bills, and even simple things like rent and groceries. But, over time, you begin to build a foundation for some stability; you're not 'under water' all the time now. You get a better job, and you have a few luxuries, a decent apartment, and can afford to go out to eat once in a while. You're just beginning to relax, when one day, your partner comes home and says, quietly and with some trepidation: "Honey, I want to talk about something . . . I've been unhappy for some time. I know I have a really great job, but I'm not happy there, and I think I want to go back to school."

From the moment you hear, "Honey I want to talk," your stomach lurches; and by the time they get to "I think I want to go back to school," your mind has already unleashed a tumult of thoughts. You're running numbers and scenarios in your head, adding up the costs and thinking of all the ways this is going to change your life, just as it is beginning to settle into some comfort. In seconds, you've come up with a host of 'good reasons' for this not being 'a good time' for going back to school.

But if you're lucky, somewhere amid the tumult, you may also hear another quiet voice inside that says: "You know, this isn't actually about *you;* the person you love is trying to tell you about what *they* need, and it's hard for them." Then, somehow, you manage to take a breath and sigh deeply before responding, "What are you going to need from me to do that, honey?" In that moment you graduate.

This is the death of the self in love. It is also the kind of self-sacrifice with which we are faced in relationships on a daily basis. Relationships demand sacrifices, and those sacrifices scare us. Sometimes we succeed in living up to the opportunity of the moment, and sometimes we fail. Often our panic speaks instead of our love, and we trample right over our partner's need and moment of vulnerability. It is a learning process, and one that we hope the relationship survives. It is sometimes difficult to gauge when to hold ground or yield space in the reciprocity of relationships, trying to meet the other's needs while getting our own needs met at the same time. But if we would just take a breath, admitting the fear while remembering the love, the response is usually going to be more holistic and better for the relationship.

The death of the self in relationships is both an opportunity and a test. If we pass the test, the love and relationship can continue to grow. If we fail, it may atrophy or begin to stagnate. For the boundless nature of love is always trying to push the boundaries of the relationship, to expand them and make them grow to accommodate its own boundless nature. This, of course, leads us to the third death.

The Death of the Beloved

The third death is the most natural, and yet, always the most difficult and unexpected for us; it is the death of the beloved, the death of the object of our love.[15]

This can be understood as the loss of a beloved through a separation *(firaq)* in life or in death, or the obscuration of the beloved in union *(wusul).*

Traditionally, Sufis have emphasized the obscuration of the *self* in union with the divine beloved. Thus, Rabi'a al-Basri says to God . . .

I have loved You with two loves—
One that is worthy of You, and one that is unworthy.
In the unworthy love, I think of You only.
In the worthy love, there is only You.[16]

In the first love, there is still a *You* and *I,* a duality and dynamic of beloved and lover. In the second, the *I* of the lover is effaced in the *You* of the beloved. Thus, when Majnun, the great lover of Persian literature, is finally reunited with his beloved Layla after years of separation, he is confused. Layla approaches him and says, "Majnun, I'm here! It is me, Layla!" But he says, "How can that be? *I am Layla!*" He is so absorbed in her that it appears there is nothing left of Majnun—there is only Layla.

And yet, this description, while approaching the threshold of union, is still in a sense participating in duality, in as much as there is a *Layla* with which to be absorbed, or any sense of *I-ness. . . . "I am Layla!"* This is more like a lover feeling into and through the experience of the beloved in love-making before *la petite mort,* 'the little death' of union itself. It is still the 'death of the self' in Ahmad Ghazzali's categories, a penultimate experience, and not yet the 'death of the beloved.'

In truth, it is really a problem of language—a *You* needs an *I* to recognize it in ordinary circumstances, suggesting duality. But when Rabi'a says, "In the worthy love, there is *only You,*" she is proposing a paradox of a *You* without an *I*. And where there is an experience of *only You,* there is actually neither *I* nor *You,* no subject or object, no self or other, only being and pure awareness. The beloved is no longer an object of longing and desire, but the *only reality,* even if just for a moment.

This is an ecstatic state that can be experienced in various ways, traditionally through *zikr* (remembrance) and *muraqaba* (meditation), weakening the ego's identification with the body in favor of the larger being. This is the goal to which much of Sufi teaching is oriented.

Ahmad Ghazzali, however, does not limit his idea of the death of the beloved to the experience of ecstatic union alone, but suggests that love is our teacher in all aspects of life, always seeking to own more and more of the territory of our lives. So how do we experience the death of the beloved in ordinary life? And how are we transformed by that experience?

Through separation and loss.

Eventually, death parts us all from the ones we love—physical deaths, deaths through separation and rejection, and even the poignant death of never fully knowing or being known by our partners. The death of the beloved is precisely that situation in which we are forced to let go of a relationship (or an aspect of it) in heartbreaking circumstances.

Tristan is willing to lose the whole world, and even suffer eternal punishment in hell for Isolde; but can he let *Isolde* go and give her up willingly? To keep her, he would surely sacrifice his own desires for her needs? But what if her need is that he sacrifice his relationship with her for the sake of her own well-being and to keep her place in society? That would be the death of the beloved.

Sometimes we are given a choice, and sometimes we are not. Either way, we lose the ones we love. The critical question for the Sufi is not *'How?'* or *'Why?'* we lose the ones we love, but *'What* remains when the beloved—the object of our love—is gone?'

The answer is . . . *Love. . . . Love liberated.*

As much as we would like to think that love and relationship are the same thing, they are not; and it is loss which teaches us this painful lesson. When the relationship with the object of our love is gone, we find that we are still in relationship with our *love,* that the love itself is bigger than the relationship. We find that it belongs to us, and we to it, and surprisingly, that it never belonged to the beloved.

Nevertheless, the love continues to crave the beauty which first set it loose in us; and in its absence, we experience pain, as if a limb had been torn from our body. It is for this reason that most people choose to *'shut it down'* and *'lock it away,'* where it can longer touch them. It is simply too painful to keep open and alive. But this, according to Sufism, is to miss the most precious opportunity of love—the experience of its pain. Rumi says . . .

> *"Oh love, everyone gives you pretty names and titles—*
> *Last night I named you again—*
> *'Pain without remedy.'"*[17]

Hazrat Inayat Khan explains, "The heart is not living until it has experienced pain,"[18] by which he means, the pain of love that awakens the heart and makes it truly sensitive to life.[19]

Rumi is even more emphatic in his *Mesnavi*—"Seek pain! Seek pain, pain, pain!"[20] In suggesting this, he is not advocating a reckless masochism, but urging lovers to be brave . . . 'Don't run from the pain of love; embrace it! Allow the love to have its way with you! It will make you grow!'

When the love is no longer bounded and held in the narrow confines of relationship, or in selfishness of any kind, however beautiful, then it can expand to its true 'dimensions.' It can be known for what it truly is in itself—*boundless!*

For the lover, the opportunity is similar, to grow and expand.

If the lover can stand firm and resist the temptation to run from the pain or bury it, transformation is possible. But if they become cynical and jaded as a mask for the pain, or learn to ignore or suppress it in distraction, there is likewise a deadening effect, a diminishment of life.[21]

We are often taught that pain is the enemy, something to be avoided at all costs. But pain is just a messenger come to tell us about the state of something else in us—a pulled muscle, a poison in the system, a broken bone, or even a broken heart. It is not always the best idea to mask or cover that message, which tends to continue as long as there is a message to be conveyed. When it is a broken bone, the message is to get it set. And after we have done that, the message is to be careful with that bone for as long as it takes to heal fully.

In the same way, emotional pain is a message which tells us the state of our hearts, and ignoring that message or masking it in some way, may actually disrupt a necessary psychological process.

I remember hearing about a woman who had lost her child in a tragic accident. She was despondent and went to her little girl's grave every day, sometimes hitting her head against the headstone until it bled. Everyone was afraid for her. Friends begged her to "take something" for the pain, but she refused. They spoke to her therapist, urging him to prescribe something for her. But he also refused. "There's nothing wrong with her," he said, "She's grieving." Her friends argued that she might harm herself. He responded with a sigh, "She might . . . But medicating her won't stop her grief; it will only mask it, and she needs to grieve."

Later, when she was able to engage the world again, she said that she had needed to grieve as deeply as she had loved. And even though the pain was nearly unbearable, it would have been a sin against the love she felt for her child if she had not allowed herself to feel her grief, completely.

The death of the beloved is both a grief process and a growth process. Both are natural, and neither should be interrupted.

Well-intentioned friends of heartbroken lovers will often say, "I wish you weren't in so much pain; you need to move on!" But this is more often an expression of their own feelings than any insight into what is actually needful in the grieving lover's process. It is not necessarily what the lover wants at all.

Yes, often, tortured by their own grief and pain, they do just that—move on as quickly as possible. But that is not what the lover's heart wants; the heart cannot even conceive of *'moving on,'* and has no desire to be parted from its pain (unless that is achieved by a reunion with the beloved). For the heart knows that the pain is born of love, and to disconnect from it, is to disconnect from that precious gift of love, too. Thus, Tristan says, "If by my 'death,' you mean the pain of this love, well that is my life!"

To keep the love—that sacred thing now liberated from the relationship, and its greatest gift—we learn to endure the pain. The pain is the price of keeping it, and its endurance tests our limits and expands our capacities for loving. It feels like it is tearing you apart, but that is only the expansion. Love is stretching you, creating a larger and larger being to hold its infinity, ruthless in its divine intent. Ultimately, love accepts no limits, and attempts to remake us in its divine image.

Thus, Hazrat Inayat Khan writes . . .

I have loved in life, and I have been loved.
I have drunk the bowl of poison from the hands of love as nectar,

and have been raised above life's joy and sorrow.
My heart, aflame in love, set afire every heart
that came in touch with it.
My heart has been rent and joined again;
My heart has been broken and again made whole;
My heart has been wounded and healed again;
A thousand deaths my heart has died,
and thanks be to love, it lives yet.
I went through hell and saw there love's raging fire,
and I entered heaven illumined with the light of love.
I wept in love and made all weep with me;
I mourned in love and pierced the hearts of all beings;
And when my fiery glance fell on the rocks,
the rocks burst forth as volcanoes.
The whole world sank in the flood caused by my one tear;
With my deep sigh the earth trembled,
and when I cried aloud the name of my beloved,
I shook the throne of God in heaven.
I bowed my head low in humility,
and on my knees I begged of love,
"Disclose to me, I pray you, love, your secret."
She took me gently by my arms and lifted me above the earth,
and spoke softly in my ear,
"My dear, you are love, lover,
and the beloved whom you have adored."[22]

muraqaba al-qalb

Meditation of the Heart

The Heart Rhythm Meditation of Sufism *

One of the most famous anecdotes about meditation in Sufism comes from the Sufi master, Abu Bakr Shibli, who said . . .

> I once saw Nuri sitting in meditation so still that not even a single hair of his body moved. So I asked him, "From whom did you learn such deep meditation?"
>
> He replied, "I learned it from a cat crouching over a mouse hole. The cat was even stiller than I!"[1]

While this may seem no more than an amusing anecdote, it actually points to what may be the single most important element in our meditation practice—*desire.* This early Sufi master, Abu'l-Husayn Nuri, asks us seriously, 'Are we as committed to our goals in meditation as a cat waiting to catch a mouse?' It is not likely. For the cat has a good reason for its focus and dedication; it wants to eat! But do we want anything half so much as a meal to keep us from starving? If we want to maintain our meditation practice, we need to know the reason we are doing it; and we need that reason to be a good one.

* An edited version of a talk originally given in Portland, Oregon on July 10th, 2016 at Lewis and Clark College for the Season of the Rose, the annual summer school of the Inayati Order.

One day, Hasan of Basra came to see Rabi'a al-Adawiyya in her meditation cell. He asked her, "Tell me about that knowledge which, untaught and unheard, came into your heart without an intermediary."

She answered, "I once spun some yarn to sell in the market in order to buy a little food. I sold it for two silver dirhams. I placed one dirham in my left hand, and the other in my right, lest they get together and overwhelm me. My victory was earned that day.[2]

It may not seem like it, but she answered him. 'What does it matter to talk about such experiences?' she suggests. 'It is better to learn how to get there.' She got there by refusing to accept any substitute for her goal. She worked to buy food to sustain her on the path, but refused to allow her two "dirhams" to conspire in tempting her to anything outside of her goal, which was nothing less than union with the divine.

Do you know what *your* goal is? Do you know that desire for which you would sacrifice short-term pleasures for long-term gains? It is something to consider.

What is Meditation?

The English word 'meditation' comes from the Latin, *meditatio,* which means, 'to measure-out thought.' The Indo-European root of the word, *me-*, means, 'measure,' and shows up in other Latin words like *medicus,* a 'doctor,' or 'someone who takes the measure of a situation,' i.e., 'diagnoses' and 'prescribes' *medicina,* 'something measured out.' So, meditation, 'to measure out thought,' is, as we might say today, 'to think about something,' or 'give thought to it.' It is basically what we mean when we talk about 'contemplation.'

You see, there is a curious swapping of meanings that has happened over time. In the Catholic Christian mystical tradition, from which we inherit the words 'meditation' and 'contemplation, *meditatio* and *contemplatio* mean the opposite of what they mean in common parlance today. *Meditatio*, or 'meditation,' refers to discursive processes, thinking into and through a sacred idea. Whereas, *contemplatio* (derived from *con-* and *templum*, describing a special focus on a 'space marked-out' as sacred, or 'gazing attentively') actually stands for what we generally think of as 'meditation' today, i.e., being absorbed, holding a one-pointed focus, or cultivating tranquility and quieting the mind.

I mention this mostly to show that the word 'meditation' can be applied in a broader way than is usually assumed (based on the more recent influences of Buddhism and Hinduism in popular culture). Thus, my own definition of 'meditation,' as a general category, might actually include both approaches, and more . . .

> Meditation is a technique or process for attuning consciousness, which—depending on the individual, the technique used, and the spiritual context in which it is done—may lead to altered states of awareness and insight, usually considered beneficial or transformative for individuals and groups.[3]

From this perspective, 'meditation' might include a variety of practices from the Sufi tradition, including: *zikr*, the mantric recitation of divine names; *fikr*, linking those names with the breath; *sama'*, 'listening' to sacred music; *muḥasaba*, reflecting on one's actions; *tafakkur*, deep contemplation; *tasawwur-i murshid*, imagining the ideal; *salah*, formal prayers; *du'a*, discursive prayer; and, of course, *muraqaba,* the meditative technique of absorbing the mind.

In many modern discussions of spiritual practice, the latter is often privileged over the others, as somehow superior. But there is no real basis for such an assumption. If it is based on the notion that meditative absorption is the highest end of practice, then it must be pointed-out that any of the aforementioned practices can lead to such states.

Each practice allows us to get at and explore different dimensions of our being and awareness, and should be equally valued for this reason. It is also good to be aware of the variety of 'tools' the tradition provides to address different ends. You may not consider yourself a 'prayer person,' but a moment may come when you need it. Likewise, you may not necessarily consider yourself a 'meditator' either, but a moment may come when you need it.

Muraqaba al-Qalb – Meditation on the Heart

But if we want to speak of 'meditation' in the more restricted, modern sense—as a technique directly cultivating meditative absorption—the Sufi term is *muraqaba*, meaning, 'to watch over' . . . Just like Nuri's cat, crouching over a mouse hole!

What does the 'cat' of our awareness watch? It watches the 'object' of its meditation. Not only in the sense of our overall purpose (though this is important, as we have already discussed), but also in the sense of one's particular focus in meditation.

According to the *kalimat-i qudsiyya* of the Khwajaghan, the eight principles of Sufi mindfulness, the breath is the vehicle we use to take us "homeward," in the direction of our source in God.[4] And where is the 'home' that houses God? In a holy tradition *(ḥadith qudsi)* from the prophet Muḥammad, God says, "I am contained in nothing except the heart which loves me."[5] Thus, the Sufis tell us . . .

Muraqaba is the presence of the heart with God,
and the absence of the heart from everything other than God.[6]

According to the great Chishti master, Shah Kalim Allah Jahanabadi, "One should focus one's full concentration upon the heart, such that all one's sensory awareness becomes unified in one direction and upon one object."[7] And uniting the two coordinates of breath and heartbeat, Hazrat Inayat Khan teaches in his *Githas* that each must be made rhythmic . . .

> Rhythm is most important in [breathing practices], for there ought to be a balance in the breath. Inhaling and exhaling must be even in rhythm [. . .][8]

And elsewhere . . .

> If there is any form of concentration to be used in meditation, it consists in first getting into the rhythm of the heart, by watching the heartbeats, feeling them and harmonizing with them.[9]

Thus, the ideal *muraqaba,* at least within Inayati Sufism, coordinates the breath with the heartbeat. We begin following the breath, as a secondary 'object' of meditation, in order to arrive at the heartbeat, the primary 'object' of our meditation.

Based on the teachings of Hazrat Inayat Khan (1882-1927), and his son Pir Vilayat Inayat Khan (1916-2004), my own meditation teacher, Pir Puran Bair (b. 1944), a senior student of Pir Vilayat, refined these teachings into a clear technique of coordinating breath and heartbeat, which he calls Heart

Rhythm Meditation, or what might also be called *muraqaba al-qalb*, 'meditation of the heart.'[10]

The Eight Elements of Posture

However, in order to establish a deep connection with the breath and heartbeat in your meditation, you have to build that meditation on a proper foundation, which is to say, a proper posture. The following are eight elements of posture to understand and implement before you start your meditation practice.[11]

1. Base: The first step is to establish your base. It is important to create a solid structure that allows you to sit up straight without much effort, or without leaning back against a support or being rigid either. Sitting up straight takes pressure off the chest and diaphragm, allowing you to breathe well and to feel your heartbeat.[12] As the spine has a natural curve to it, it is actually important to angle your thighs down by some means so as to accommodate that curve, which in turn allows for a naturally straight back. You can do this by using an appropriate posture, a bolster, or meditation bench. If you are sitting in a chair, come to the edge of the seat, allowing your knees and thighs to angle downward.[13] Then, feel the earthy weight of your body in this posture and experience its deep stillness.

2. Arms: Next consider the position of your arms and hands. If your base is allowing you to sit up straight, your arms should drop naturally from your shoulders, allowing room for your lungs to expand. Thus, in finding a place for your hands to settle, you do not want to do anything to crowd your rib cage. Sometimes a particular hand position is recommended, as when a Sufi places the right palm on the left thigh and takes the right wrist in the left hand.[14] Nevertheless, one should still do this in such a way as to allow for unimpeded breathing.

3. Upward: Now, inhale and stretch your shoulders upward, as if you are trying to touch your ears with them.[15]

4. Inward: While your shoulders are up, inhale deeper, and pull them back so that the shoulder blades meet in the center of your back.[16]

5. Head: Now, exhale and allow your shoulders to relax and settle into a naturally "royal pose,"[17] with your chest out and the back of your head drawn upward, the chin tucked slightly. When your chin is up, there is no strength in your posture.

There is wisdom in these last three steps, which may not be immediately apparent. I have never forgotten how skillfully Pir Puran demonstrated the fact that "relaxation follows tension." If you tell people to 'sit up straight,' they tend to do something fairly artificial that looks too rigid and not quite right. It is difficult for them to find 'straight.' But when you inhale and take your shoulders too high and too far back, and then release them with an exhalation, you will find that you come into a natural posture of dignity, which is important for us to experience.

6. Mouth: Your mouth should be natural, lips neither pursed or open. With your jaw unclenched, keep the tongue in the area of your upper teeth where it settles naturally.

7. Eyes: You can either close your eyes or keep them open; but if you keep them open, make sure they are not focused, but held in a soft gaze.

8. Breath: Finally, breathe out through the nose. As Pir Vilayat would say, "Always begin your practice with the outbreath."[18] Your breath on both the inhalation and exhalation should be deep, easy, smooth, and quiet.

In the course of your meditation, you may find that your posture has slackened or become a little too relaxed. When this happens, do not hurry to correct it or become overly critical of yourself; simply repeat elements three and four with an inhalation, then element five with an exhalation, and return to your meditation.

The point of good posture is to reduce the number of distractions that come from your body, disturbing your meditation. If a posture is comfortable and easy to maintain in stillness, you will be able to hold the object of your meditation much better. In fact, if you keep your body still for long enough, for approximately twenty minutes, your "pressure sense" will turn off.[19] If your hands are on your legs, they generally feel the separation between hands and thighs, the heat of both, and a sensory exchange. But after about twenty minutes, the body "will feel monolithic, undifferentiated,"[20] like a resin molded statue of a body in seated meditation. You can see the hands and arms and legs, but they are actually just surface distinctions in one molded body.

The secret behind the almost universally recommended '20-30 minutes' of meditation is largely based on this observation of when the senses begin to withdraw. At this point, the body achieves a more or less stable state allowing for undistracted meditation.

The Process of Heart Rhythm Meditation

Now Heart Rhythm Meditation, or *muraqaba al-qalb*, is not a technique to be applied quickly, but rather, a structured process for coming into a relationship with the breath and heartbeat, gradually allowing one to coordinate the two. That process begins with simply becoming conscious of the breath and its patterns.

Conscious Breath: Begin to watch your breath. Be conscious of every inhalation and exhalation. Make no effort to change the way you breathe; just notice the breath as it is, with the rhythm set by the unconscious.[21] Notice how it lifts your chest, and feel its delicacy as it enters and leaves your nostrils.

You may even notice that it has four phases: a 'rising' inhalation; a 'top' where the breath is retained; a 'descending' exhalation; and a 'bottom' before the next inhalation.

Watch these four phases as they happen. Notice the natural length of each for you, counting the rising inhalation . . . *1, 2, 3, 4,* etc., paying attention to whether you hold your breath at the top, then counting the descending exhalation as well . . . *1, 2, 3, 4,* etc., and finally, noting whether you hold your breath at the bottom.[22]

Some people will hold their breath at the top, or pause briefly there; and some will hold their breath at the bottom, or likewise, pause there, briefly. For some people, the breath might be long and deep . . . *1, 2, 3, 4, 5, 6, 7, 8,* and for others, short and staccato . . . *1, 2, 3.* Sometimes a person will even notice that their inhalation and exhalation are of different lengths. All of this is simply information, and not to be judged. And yet, we may view it as a diagnostic possibly reflecting our unconscious view of life and how we are feeling in life.[23]

For instance, if you are holding at the bottom, when your lungs are empty, it is worth asking yourself—'Why am I waiting to take a new breath? The body wants to breathe, after all, so why am I holding my breath?'

Likewise, differing lengths for the inhalation and exhalation may also tell us something about how we feel or think about certain things; perhaps a need for energy or personal safety, or a need to rest or provide assurance. It is not as simple as that, of course, but it gives you an idea of how you might consider the information as it is given to you.

This is the first stage: coming into a relationship with our breath, and making it conscious. Or as the Khwajaghan put it, *hosh dar dam!* 'mind on the breath!'

Rhythmic Breath: The next stage is to make the breath rhythmic, to get it into a rhythm, *nazar bar qadam!* 'watch your steps!'

In as much as our breathing patterns may reflect our emotional states and unconscious views, they may also affect and perpetuate them. After all, we know for certain that our emotions can have a deleterious effect on our bodies; but how often do we consider how that same connection might allow our bodies to positively affect our emotions?[24] If we adjust and balance those same breathing patterns (which may have indicated some emotional disharmony in us), making them even and rhythmic, we might also balance the emotional states connected to them.

As a model of rhythmic motion, consider the pendulum, or the swing. Visualize the breath moving away from your heart with the exhalation in a swinging or pendular movement, and returning to your heart in the same way with the inhalation. As you breathe out, the breath carries the swing away from you. As you breathe in, the breath draws the swing back to you. As the swing comes back on the inhalation, it will settle momentarily in the heart-center, naturally bringing you a greater awareness of your heartbeat. We call this 'swinging the breath.'[25]

Now begin to count the length of your inhalations and exhalations, gradually evening them out to the same length. This will balance your breath and make your heart rate rhythmic. Keep your breath quiet and smooth.[26]

Do not expect your mind to be free of thoughts. If you find that you have become lost in them for a moment, just return to counting your inhalations and exhalations as you swing the breath . . . *1, 2, 3, 4, 5, 6,* etc.

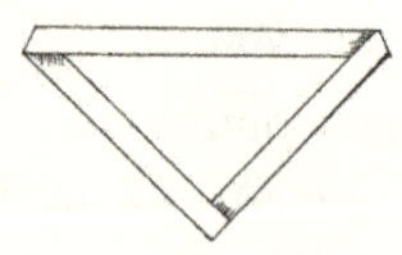

Full Breath: Though we may feel a lot of comfort in this breathing rhythm, it is likely that we are not actually breathing at our capacity yet. Most of us tend to breathe shallow, high up in the chest. But if you were to place a baby on its back and observe its breathing, you would see that it breathes deeply from its belly, not shallow in its chest.[27]

Why does our breathing change from its naturally deep and full pattern? It is probably a response to repeated stresses. Nevertheless, a natural inhalation fills up from the belly, or the bottom of the lungs, and only rises into the chest after. Likewise, a natural exhalation should reverse the process, the chest depressing first and the bottom of the lungs after. That is a full breath.

But, in order to get a truly full breath and inhalation, you first need to make a full exhalation. This is a problem for many of us, because it requires that we press the diaphragm back at the bottom of our exhalation in order to empty our lungs fully.[28] There is an inherent fear in doing this because, in contacting that place of emptiness, it feels as if we are 'touching death.' The word *expire* means both 'to die' and 'to breathe out.' Thus, we seem to be breathing shallow in order to conserve that extra air in the bottom of our lungs, as if we could preserve our lives with it. In the meantime, however, we are not actually living our lives, at least not fully.[29]

Perhaps the most famous of Sufi maxims comes from a *ḥadith* (report) of the prophet Muḥammad, who tells us, *mutu qabla an tamutu,* 'die before death.' Or, as my dear friend, the former Carmelite Christian abbess, Tessa Bielecki, is wont to say, "It is my experience that people do not experience 'resurrection' enough because they don't let themselves *die dead enough* . . . we don't experience all the life that is waiting for us because we don't have the courage to die."[30]

Just as we cannot live fully until we have fully embraced our mortality, we cannot breathe fully until we have exhaled fully, risking that 'little death' for the sake of 'more life.'[31] For that is exactly what happens when we have the courage to 'expire,' pressing the last bit of air from the bottom of our lungs—oxygen floods back into them, filling them completely, top to bottom, and we experience a "rush of energy," new inspiration. The word *inspire* means both 'to animate' and 'to breathe in.'[32]

So after spending the first part of our meditation period in conscious, rhythmic breathing, we attempt a period of full exhalation and full inhalation. Relaxing your chest, you breathe-out easily according to your normal count, then contract your diaphragm muscle to exhale an extra count of three to finish the exhalation and empty your lungs completely.[33] If, for instance, your normal exhalation count is consistently four, it will likely lengthen to seven.

Never hold your breath at the end of the exhalation, but begin the inhalation as soon as the exhalation is complete. Inhale deeply, at a length roughly equal to your full exhalation. Relax your diaphragm and allow your belly to expand like a balloon, rising into your chest and pushing it outward. With each inhalation, your stomach should fill visibly and your chest should rise. Think of the in-breath as rising energy.[34]

You should limit the number of breaths you take this way to about ten, as this is only a stage in the Heart Rhythm Meditation process, and you do not want to hyperventilate.[35] This will be enough to demonstrate your capacity for breathing fully.

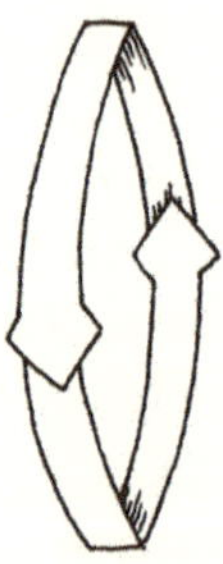

Retention: In each phase of the practice, we are making small interventions in our breathing process. We began by making it conscious, then even and rhythmic, and then full. In the Yoga tradition, such interventions are grouped under the term, *pranayama,* 'controlling the breath.' In Sufism, the parallel term is *pas-i anfas,* 'observing the breaths.'[36]

The final intervention we make in this lineage of practice is a long retention at the top of the breath when the lungs are full. We first learned this retention in the older Chishti *qasab* practice, holding the breath twice the length of our inhalation. But we can also do it with our meditation practice. When your lungs are full, you have the basic capacity to hold your breath for approximately twice the length of the in-breath you have just taken. If it is an inhalation to a count of four . . . *1, 2, 3, 4,* it becomes a retention count of eight . . . *1, 2, 3, 4, 5, 6, 7, 8* at the top.[37]

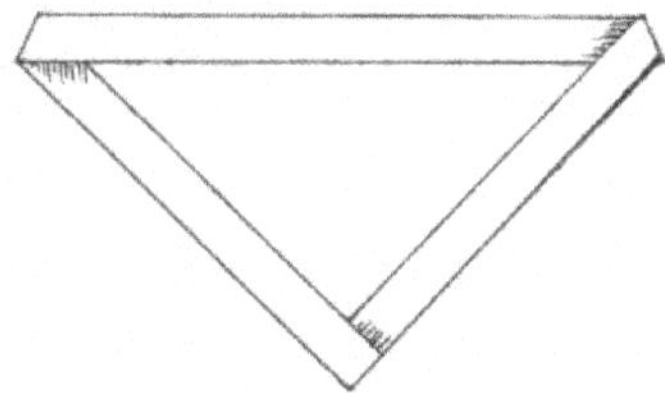

Although this may seem to suggest a geometric structure reminiscent of an inverted isosceles triangle, Hazrat Inayat Khan, an Indian classical musician, actually thinks of this breathing pattern in terms of a four-part rhythm, describing what I tend to think of as the diamond structure of Heart Rhythm Meditation.[38]

> Rhythm is most important in [breathing practices], for there ought to be a balance in the breath. Inhaling and exhaling must be even in rhythm, but the holding of the breath should not necessarily be even with the rhythm of inhaling and exhaling. For [...] three bars make a

> phrase or sentence of music odd in rhythm; to make it even, four bars are required. Therefore, the holding should balance evenly with inhaling and exhaling both, in order to make it four bars.[39]

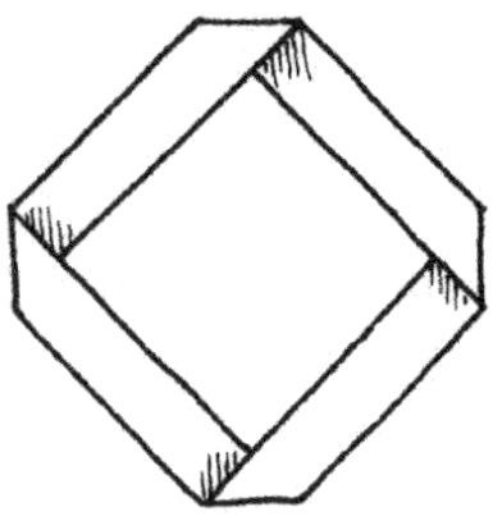

After a good inhalation, when your lungs are full of air, try holding your breath for double the count of your inhalation. While holding it, pay attention and see if you can feel your heartbeat in your chest.

We hold the breath because the sound and movement of our breathing tends to mask the heartbeat, as Shah Kalim Allah points out in his *Kashkul-i Kalimi* . . .

> Sometimes it happens that the flow of breathing obscures one's ability to hear this vibration. To prevent this, the breath should be suspended [...] In this way, the heart becomes like water, tranquil in a basin, that is preserved from being obscured by any waves or agitation and therefore can reflect the image of something other than itself.[40]

The longer you hold the breath, the 'louder' your heartbeat will be, until, eventually, you will even be able to count by it. Holding your breath in this way will expand the heart magnetically, and you will feel the power of it in your chest.

Nevertheless, do not hold the breath longer than double the length of your inhalation. Double the length is enough to challenge your fears and to experience the heartbeat.[41] Again, Shah Kalim Allah echoes this same sentiment, adding an exhortation to continue the practice . . .

> One should be careful not to suspend the breath to such an extent that one becomes deadly sick. Still, the danger of suspending the breath is less than the danger of never suspending it. Suspending the breath should be done according to one's own capacity. And when the suspending breath is exhaled, it should be released gradually and gently, and during exhaling also one should pay close attention to one's heart vibration.[42]

And elsewhere . . .

> Then one knows by experience that the flesh of the heart is moving with a vibration that says *['Allah']*. When one has been blessed with this happiness, then one can summon the spiritual aspiration to listen—whether alone or in the company of others—for the silent speech of one's own heart. At this point, one realizes that the heart is perpetually meditating on God by repeating the name *[Allah]*.[43]

For the Sufi, the doubled beats, or universal *'lub-dub'* of the heart, seem to be saying, *'A-llah, A-llah, A-llah, A-llah,'* reciting a natural two-syllabled *zikr,* a primordial vibratory refrain echoed throughout creation. To hear this refrain, and to listen to it actively in *muraqaba al-qalb,* is another form of *zikr khafi,* the 'hidden' or 'silent *zikr.'* For this reason, the retention of the breath in this way, allowing for an experience of the heartbeat, is a highly regarded practice among Sufis. So much so that the famous Sufi prince, Dara Shikuh, writes in his *Risala-i Haqq-Numa* . . .

> The method of spiritual practice which has been adopted by this lowly seeker is the suspension of breath *(habs-i nafas)*. I have found this method to be the best and choicest method, without which success cannot be obtained. So everyone ought to practice this method of suspending the breath.[44]

Diamond Breath: Having established the *Conscious Breath,* the *Rhythmic Breath,* and the *Full Breath,* incorporating *Retention,* we begin our practice of the *Diamond Breath*[45] of Heart Rhythm Meditation in earnest . . .

> *1. Full Exhalation:* Breathe out easily by relaxing your chest, then by squeezing your diaphragm muscle. Use the last three heartbeats to complete the exhalation and empty your lungs. Never hold your breath at the end of the exhalation, but begin the inhalation as soon as the exhalation is complete.
>
> *2. Full Inhalation:* Breathe in first by relaxing your diaphragm, allowing your belly to extend like a balloon that fills with air, expanding your chest outward. With each inhalation, the stomach area should move visibly out. Think of the in-breath as rising energy.
>
> *3. Retention:* After your lungs are full of air, pause and hold your inhalation (never your exhalation). Hold the inhalation the length of the full exhalation.
>
> *4. Retention:* Continue holding the inhalation until you have reached a count doubling the length of the full exhalation. This slows down the breathing cycle and prevents hyperventilation.

A cycle of ten such breaths is considered a benchmark accomplishment. If any part of the cycle is too long or too short, simply adjust the cycle to one of the following patterns:

4-8-4, 5-10-5, 6-12-6, 7-14-7, 8-16-8, 9-18-9, 10-20-10.[46]

Though sometimes difficult for the beginner to maintain at first, this breathing rhythm eventually becomes second nature, and more than a mere tool of concentration. Over time, it is possible to build a profound relationship with the heartbeat, a relationship which continues beyond the period of meditation, and even beyond the boundaries of the body, extending into the universe. Through it, one comes to know the truth in the little known *ḥadith* of the prophet Muḥammad, quoted by Khwaja Mu'in ad-Din Chishti, the founder of the Chishti lineage . . .

"The hearts of the faithful are the very throne of God.
Thus, one must make a pilgrimage to the ka'bah of the heart."[47]

wahdat al-wujud

The Unity of All Being

An Introduction to the Sufi Path of Knowledge *

Muhyiddin ibn 'Arabi tells a story of a great Sufi he met while traveling through Tunis, a poor fisherman living in seclusion in a marsh with whom he stayed for three days. The fisherman prayed both day and night, though every morning he went out fishing, always catching three fish. One he would let go, one he gave to the poor, and one was his meal for the day.

When Ibn 'Arabi was ready to take his leave, the fisherman asked him where he was going.

"Egypt," he replied.

Then tears came into the fisherman's eyes, and he said: "My *shaykh* is in Egypt! Please, if you would, pay my respects, and ask him what I am to do in the world."

Though the man seemed to need no guidance, Ibn 'Arabi agreed to seek out his *shaykh*.

When Ibn 'Arabi reached Egypt, he found the *shaykh* living in a palace filled with wealth and luxury. He seemed to be merely a worldly man! But when he told the *shaykh* the request of his student in Tunis, the *shaykh* replied: "Tell him to take the love of this world out of his heart."

---

* An edited version of a talk originally given in Boulder, Colorado, on March 17th, 2019, at Naropa University, "Caring for the World: Integrating the Dual and Non-Dual Path of Awakening" with Pir Shabda Kahn, and a later talk in Boulder, Colorado, on January 9th, 2020, at Naropa University, Sufi Retreat Intensive.

This seemed an amazing statement coming from a man who lived in a palace; but when Ibn 'Arabi returned to Tunis and told this to the poor fisherman, the man began to sob and said: "For thirty years I have tried to take the love of the world out of my heart; and yet, I am still a worldly man! At the same time, my master lives amid riches and hasn't a drop of it in his heart—neither the love of it, nor the fear of it. That is the difference between him and me!"[1]

One man lives in poverty and seems the very embodiment of ascetic spirituality; another lives amid wealth and comfort and is assumed to be a "worldly man"; but the appearances are deceiving. We tend to call one thing *'sacred'* and another *'profane,'* often for fairly arbitrary reasons. But what is essentially *'profane'* about the world and materiality? And what is essentially *'sacred'* about its absence and the rejection of it? It is a judgment based on an ascetic separation of 'matter and spirit,' a dualistic view of the universe that was especially prevalent in Classical and Late Antiquity (8th-century B.C.E. to 6th-century C.E.). Matter was assigned a negative value for seeming to 'imprison the spirit,' which was associated with everything immaterial, and thus positive. But, as the wise Bard once noted of such prisons, "there is nothing either good or bad, but thinking makes it so."[2] In which case, the 'profane' is but the misapprehension and consequent misuse of the inherently sacred.

Muhyiddin ibn 'Arabi (1165-1240), who tells of these two men, is called among Sufis the *shaykh al-akbar*, or the 'greatest *shaykh,'* being perhaps the most profound map-maker of the inner terrain in all of Sufism. Born in Al-Andalus, or Muslim Spain, he traveled widely through North Africa, Egypt,

Palestine, Syria, Arabia, Iraq, and Anatolia, before finally settling in Damascus, dying at the age of seventy-five. A genius of remarkable productivity, some 800 works are attributed to him. Among them are a beautiful volume of love poetry *Turjuman al-Ashwaq* (Translator of Desires), the thirty-seven volume masterpiece *Futuhat al-Makkiyya* (Meccan Illuminations), a slim treatise on non-duality *Risalat al-Wujudiyya* (Message on Being), and the classic *Fusus al-Hikam* (Bezels of Wisdom).

In these latter works, we find the most profound ideas of the Sufi 'school of knowledge,' a somewhat artificial designation which, nevertheless, describes a certain emphasis on the intellectual understanding of various profound metaphysical concepts in Sufism—among them, the 'Gods of belief' and the 'unity of all being.'

The Gods of Belief

In the *Fusus al-Hikam,* we find examples of Ibn 'Arabi's beautifully described concept of the 'Gods of belief.' These are the true idols to be broken. It is not idols of clay that harm us as human beings, but the idols of the mind that distract us from and divide the truth.

According to Ibn 'Arabi, as God necessarily transcends all limited names and forms, the heart of the ordinary human being cannot see or know God as such, but only the 'God of their belief,' the 'God' of which they have formed a limited idea (according to their capacity), that idea conforming to what has been revealed to them *from God,* who has also determined what the content of that belief should be![3] Or, in Ibn 'Arabi's own words . . .

> The Gods of belief are subject to certain limitations, and it is these Gods that are contained in the servant's

> heart, since the absolute God cannot be contained by anything, being the very essence of everything, and of itself.[4]

And elsewhere, he writes . . .

> This is the God of belief, which varies according to the predisposition inherent in a particular person; as al-Junayd said, when asked about the knowledge of God and the knower, "The color of the water is the same as that of its container," which is a very precise answer, showing the matter as it is.[5]

Thus, beliefs regarding God necessarily differ from one person to another, each forming a single facet of what God actually *is*. However, while such beliefs can never be faithful to the divine truth, they are nonetheless also *'God revealed by God'* at the very same time![6] In a curious way, God is actually responsible for our differences regarding God . . .

> The god of one believer has no validity in respect to the god of one who believes something else. The supporter of a particular belief defends what they believe and champions it, while that which they believe in does not support them! It is because of this that they can have no effect on their opponent's belief. Thus, also, their opponent derives no assistance from their own god formulated in belief. . . . *They have no helpers.* This is because reality has denied to the gods of creedal formulations any possibility of rendering assistance, since each one is restricted to itself. Both the one assisted and the one who assists are in truth the totality ...[7]

This reminds me of the famous "Meditation on Divine Will," recorded in the midst of our terrible civil war, where "Father Abraham" reflects to himself in a private moment, "The will of God prevails. In great contests each party claims to act in accordance with the will of God … it is quite possible that God's purpose is something different from the purpose of either party." The summation of his thought is the beginning of his meditation—either way, whatever our 'Gods of belief' might tell us, "The will of God prevails."[8]

A human being attempting to know God, "the totality," is like a cell trying to describe the body. How can a cell know what the body is, either the greater shape of that body, or its life? It might contain the pattern of the whole, being a 'fractal' of the body in some sense, and it might know itself *as* the body, being part and parcel of the whole, but how much can it really know of the whole body? The lesser cannot comprehend the greater.

Thus, the ordinary human being cannot know or describe God, "the totality," but only the God of their belief, the God of which they have formed an idea.[9] We can only know that which conforms to what has been revealed to us from God, either in our predispositions, or in everything we have learned up to that point. When God is "all and everything,"[10] all conceptions of God, and all denials of God, are likewise from God.

Each of us has a "facet" of the truth, but none of us have the truth itself. That is our situation. Thus, the ultimate thing to know as a human being is that your knowledge is limited. To know that *you do not know* is the acme of knowledge. It is knowledge-based humility, and humility is wisdom. Humility makes space where knowing takes it up. We must know that the Gods of our belief, though uniquely ours, are also idols. In this way, we actually come closer to God through knowing our ignorance.

The Unity of All Being

As interesting as the idea of the 'Gods of belief' may be in itself, it is clearly dependent on a radical view of non-duality. Among Sufis, this view espoused by Ibn 'Arabi is called *waḥdat al-wujud*, the 'unity of being' or 'existence,' a phrase encapsulating a potentially 'game-changing' perspective for the Sufi initiate, and one which is often considered a great secret.

I once attended an Arab-Pakistani wedding reception in the Thayer Hotel in New York. The ballroom thundered with music, the Palestinian Arabs dancing *debke,* and the Pakistanis dancing with arms in the air to their favorite Bollywood music. Neither Pakistani nor Arab myself, I stood out somewhat in the crowd, with my fair skin and reddish-brown hair and beard; but both the Arabs and Pakistanis seemed to assume, almost automatically, that I was a Turk and quickly accepted me as such. By interesting chance, I was seated at a table next to the only other Sufi in the room—another Chishti Sufi, but from Pakistan. It turned out that he was also a *khalifa,* and he began to question me about my morning practices, and to tell me about his. Upon asking about the contexts in which I taught in the United States, and hearing that I taught Sufism publically, he looked very surprised. After considering this for a moment, he leaned in close, close enough so that no one else could hear, and asked me, "And . . . do you teach them about . . . *waḥdat al-wujud?"*

"Yes," I answered.

"And do they . . . *understand?"*

"Some . . . Some intellectually, and a few, in truth."

His questions marked the difference in our cultures: his in which such a view is held as precious by Sufis, while bordering on heresy to the majority; and mine in which it is acceptable for Sufis to discuss such things publically, but where very little is treated as precious. In both cultures, however, one thing remains the same: the *'secret'* remains a secret until it is experienced and integrated, whether understood intellectually, or not.

But if we were actually to live in-line with Ibn 'Arabi's unitive vision of reality, or at least our notion of it—while still maintaining a qualified sense of separate identity—then we might speak of our awareness of God as the "only being" as Shah Kalim Allah Jahanabadi does in the introduction to his *Kashkul-i Kalimi* . . .

> *"All praises be to God—from God, to God, and for God alone.*[11] *[...]*
> *We ask God to always ask God for nothing but God!"*[12]

That is to say, our qualified sense of separate identity asks the God-reality *that we are in truth*, to always ask of itself, for nothing but itself! For we must first confess our sense of 'I-ness' in order to move from it into other dimensions of knowing and being.

It is a wrestling match with paradox that eventually breaks open the ordinary mind. This is part of the genius of Ibn 'Arabi's presentation: he leaves us nowhere to go, no escape. He demands a stressful confrontation with the truth which, if maintained, leads to a breakthrough in consciousness, much like a Zen *koan.*

And yet, he is only taking the view of God as expressed in the Qur'an *al-Karim* to its logical conclusions. In fact, he might say, the non-dual perspective of God is the only acceptable view for the Muslim based on the Qur'an (6:103) itself . . .

> *"No vision can grasp God, but God's grasp is over all vision.*
> *God is above all comprehension, yet acquainted with all things."*

Again, what can the cell know of the body? We may be *comprehended*—'caught hold of' and encompassed—by God, "the totality," but we cannot *comprehend* or encompass God in the same way. God is "acquainted with all things" by being all things. If the ego, as a separate identity, could encompass God in thought, then the ego would be God!

This, of course, is how the jurists interpreted Mansur al-Hallaj's infamous utterance, *An al-Haqq!* 'I am the Truth!' They believed he was identifying God with his ego; but he was actually saying his ego had been obscured by God!

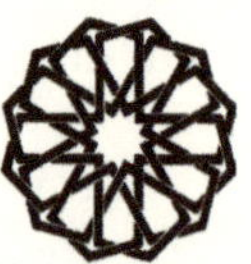

Bayazid Bistami, in a classic Sufi anecdote, says in a moment of ecstasy during *zikr,* "Glory be to me!" Horrifying his Sufis!

Later, when the master was sober again, the murids approached him and said, "Master, *ummm* . . . in the *zikr,* you shouted, "Glory be to me!"

To which he exclaimed, "God forbid I said that! I did no such thing!"

The next *zikr,* he again cried out, "Glory be to me!"

The murids approached him once more, "Master, you did it again."

"God forbid I should say such a thing! . . . If I do that again, I want you to take out your daggers and slay me for such an offence!"

The next week—"Glory be to me!"

Dutifully, the murids draw their daggers and thrust them into the master. Immediately, they are seized with sharp pain and find themselves bleeding while Bistami is completely unharmed![13]

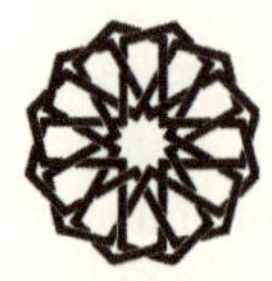

"God forbid *'I'* should say such a thing!" was correct. His "I" said nothing; it was God speaking, not Bistami; and there is no harming God without harming ourselves. The 'little i' does not comprehend the 'great I'; it is the 'great eye' that looks through the 'small eye.'

Elsewhere in the Qur'an (2:163) we are told . . .

"And your God is one God.
There is no God but God."

This is the statement of God's *tawḥid,* or 'unity.' "God is one God" . . . not two, not three. What does that mean? We might say, 'I am one person, and you are another, and you, over there, you are still another.' But not so here; God is 'one without a second,' without another . . . any other. For it says, "There is no God but God."

"God forgives not that partners should be associated with God;
God forgives everything else as God wills;
but to associate partners with God
is to craft a tremendous sin."

Based on these indications from the Qur'an (4:48), and others in which God speaks about the evil of 'associating partners' with God, Muslim theologians derived the heresy of *shirk,* 'association.'[14] *Shirk* is associating any other power with God, or suggesting that anything has power other than God, because that would suggest that there is a power that is not God's, and thus that God's power is somehow limited. Based on this notion of *shirk,* Ibn 'Arabi's conclusions are nearly inescapable: God is the "only being; there is nothing else."[15]

Let's explore some of the more important statements and passages from Ibn 'Arabi's beautiful little treatise (little more than twenty pages) on non-duality, *Risalat al-Wujudiyya,* the 'message on being.'

"God is visible in all that is seen."[16]

This is almost a meditation in itself. Imagine you are reading these very words and, as their import lands, you think, 'But my eyes are open! How then can I be failing to see God?' The answer is, you are not failing to see God. It is only that you are not convinced it is God before you. As it says in the Qur'an: "And wherever you turn, there is God's face. Truly God is omnipresent, omniscient." (2:115)

"God is neither inside nor outside of anything."[17]

With this one statement, Ibn 'Arabi' dispenses with the notions of panentheism, panpsychism, and theism: God is not 'in all things,' 'the soul in them,' or 'outside' the material universe. God is neither *'out there,'* nor *'in here.'* There is no 'inside' or 'outside' with God, because God is both sides, simultaneously.

"None can conceive of God
through the senses or the mind, knowledge or imagination. . . .
Only God can see God; only God can conceive God."[18]

Ibn 'Arabi is taking things away from us. We are not going to conceive God with our minds. The mind cannot really conceive the unity of all being, but it keeps trying. Instead, it creates penultimate mental structures, concepts. We trick ourselves into believing these conceptions of non-duality are the realization of the non-dual; but they are not. When the mind stops the mental gymnastics—trying to hold God, conceive God—then *God.* God is simply present, *simply is,* and never was not. We do not think *about* God . . . *God—that's it.* "Only God can see God; only God can conceive God."

"That which hides God is God's oneness."[19]

"God's oneness" is self-protecting; it is inaccessible to the mind and thus hides itself from us. There is only one door, one lock, one key . . . *experience.* We are still looking for a 'something' called "oneness." But the oneness "is neither inside nor outside." God is simply there, hidden in plain sight. All the 'names and forms' of this world, all the minutiae and apparently separate parts, narrow our focus, shifting our awareness from the totality, or the whole, and thus hide God from us. And yet, all the 'names and forms' that hide God are also God's oneness, their 'separateness' merely an appearance.

"No prophet sent to the people, no saint,
not the perfected, nor an angel near to the
throne in heaven can see God,
for they are not apart from God."[20]

That is to say, while separated into the identities of prophet, saint, perfected being, or angel, it is not possible to see God; only when these identities yield to the truth of their inherent divinity can God be 'seen.' "Only God can see God."

If God is "neither inside nor outside of anything," how could they see God? 'Seeing' in the ordinary sense requires object relations, separation of one sort or another between the seer and the seen. It requires a removal of God to a location where God might be 'seen.' But where is God's locus? Perhaps the best answer we can give to that question is this: "God is an infinite sphere whose circumference is *nowhere,* and whose center is *everywhere.*"[21]

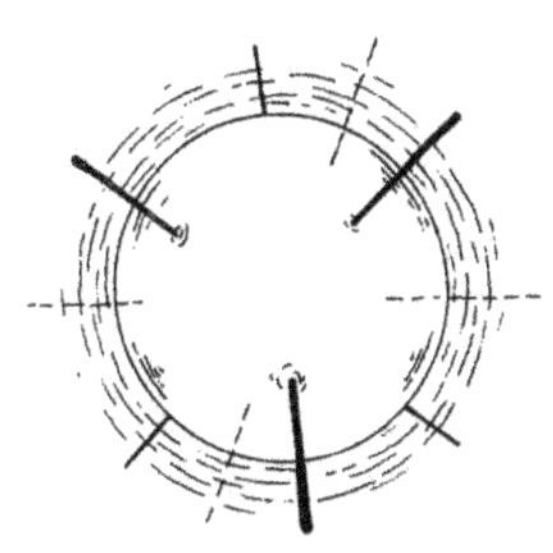

This *'almost'* of the mind is the best we can do with the mind. You can conceive a sphere, but you will never see its infinity; you can imagine a center, but not everywhere; for it is *here, here, here, and here, ad infinitum* . . . It overwhelms the mind. It is merely an abstraction with enough elements of the concrete to provide us with a penultimate idea of God's infinite wholeness, and yet, it still is not God, nor a knowledge of God.

"God sent God's essence from God's essence,
through God's essence, to God's essence.
There is no difference between the sender and the sent."[22]

Think about it—the message does not even travel!

Such radical conclusions are likely part of the reason a garbage dump was later established over Ibn 'Arabi's grave in Damascus.[23] If there is really no difference between the sender, the sent, and the receiver, then the message of God, the prophet, the people, and even Satan and all that is rejected as base and unworthy—alcohol and gambling, saint and sinner—are equally "God's essence," not more or less holy! There is no difference in essence. For those who base their lives on such differences, this is more than disconcerting; it is an untenable heresy.

> If you believe that things exist *in* God—*from* God, or *with* God—or that anything depends on God for its existence, then those things are as gods to you. Even if you believe their power derives from God, that belief is heresy, for that is something apart and separate from God, a partner with God. It would be a mistake to think of any existence as valid beside the existence of God, even if that existence is seen as dependent.[24]

Attributing reality to anything other than God is saying that this 'reality' has a power; and since God is theologically 'all-powerful,' this is idolatry. If I say, 'I have the *power* to open the door,' this is a heresy to non-duality, suggesting that the power is mine and not God's. If say, "I am going to open the door," this, too, is a heresy. Thus, we say, *'insha-Allah,* 'God willing,' first, because it is hubris to think that 'I' do anything!

"All the world's a stage" and God is playing all the parts . . . and the stage, too.[25] Thus, believing that God created the world and human beings is *shirk.* Even if you say they exist as dependent beings, receiving all their power from God, it is still *shirk.* "There is one God; nothing else exists."[26] There can be nothing else, or else God is limited in some way. Even if we take up the smallest sliver of space in the universe, God occupying all the rest, it still means that there is something *not-God,* and thus a power beside or in opposition to God.

Ibn 'Arabi' then quotes and explains a *ḥadith* (report) of the prophet Muḥammad held sacred in the Sufi tradition . . .

> "To know oneself is to know your sustainer (God)."[27] By this is meant that you are not you, and you—without really knowing it—are God. God is not within you, and you are not within God. [...] When you are addressed as you, do not fool yourself that you exist with an independent essence and qualities and attributes—for you do not exist, never existed, nor ever will. You have not entered God, nor God entered you. [...] Without an identity, you are God and God is you. If you know yourself as nothing, then you know your sustainer; otherwise, you know not.[28]

Only when you know yourself as *not-you* will you know God. Take the 'label' off. The spiritual path is not a path of knowing more and more; it is a path of unknowing, unwinding all the things we think we know about ourselves.

Many years ago, when one of my teachers who first introduced me to non-dual philosophies was still in college, he was at a party where a friend said to him, "You know, there is an Indian sage in the bedroom!" Curious, he knocks on the door of the bedroom and enters. There, indeed, is an Indian sage seated on the floor in meditation posture. So he sits down on the floor in front of him and the sage asks him in a pidgin English, "Who you?"

"Oh," he says, "I'm John . . ."

"No," the sage interrupts, "family name." That is a name you were given. "Who you?"

"I'm a student here at the university, studying . . ."

"No . . . occupation." That is what you are doing; it is a societal name. "Who you?"

Now, finally catching on, he says, "I am the immortal *atman,*" the immortal self identical with God.

"Book name," says the sage. "Who you?"

Finally, he sighs and says, "I don't know . . ."

"Find out."[29]

And that was the end of the interview.

When we begin to remove the labels, we become more and more the "sphere whose circumference is nowhere."

Ibn 'Arabi continues . . .

> And yet, you cannot know your sustainer by making yourself nothing. Many of the wise claim that one must remove the signs of one's existence, efface one's identity, and rid oneself of the self to know one's sustainer. But this is a mistake. How could that which does not exist rid itself of its existence? There is nothing with inherent existence, so how could something that is not become nothing? Only something can become nothing. However, if you know yourself to be without inherent

> existence, not trying to become nothing, then you may know God, your sustainer.[30]

There are many teachers who will tell you that you have to 'make yourself nothing,' saying, 'Get rid of Netanel! Get rid of your possessions! Get rid of your identity!' But not Ibn 'Arabi. He says, "How could that which does not exist rid itself of its existence?" Talk of independent 'existence,' or an independent 'identity,' implies that something separate and independent somehow came into being and will at some point cease to exist; but nothing of the kind ever happened, as this kind of separation does not actually exist; we are radically interdependent beings, integrated with our environments, outgrowths of those environments, never truly separated or separable from them.

Allow me to give you an example.

Think of a tree. Is there any tree without the earth in which it is rooted, without the nutrients in the soil that nourish it, without a source of water, or without sunlight? Does any tree grow without these ingredients? *No.* The 'tree' which is separable from these constituent 'parts' is an abstraction, only existing in the mind, or for a brief moment after being uprooted from its environment.

Now, if a tree does not exist apart from the earth, water, nutrients, and light it needs, then where does the 'tree' really begin or end? Is the 'tree' not also, in some sense, the water, the earth, the nutrients, the microbial life it interacts with, the things that live upon it, the sun, and the oxygen?

And we could ask the same question about ourselves. Where do we start, and where do we end? Is our skin the outer limit of our being? Like the trees, we need oxygen for respiration. We need sunlight for Vitamin D. More than half of our diet comes from fruits and vegetables from the earth, and includes bacteria from the soil aiding good digestion. And we cannot live without water much more than three days. Are we not, then, in some sense, water, light, and earth, too? Are we not simply another outgrowth of the planet? As Alan Watts so beautifully put it . . . Just as the apple tree "*apples*"—making apples—the planet "*peoples*"—making human beings![31]

Moreover, there is no human being without other human beings, and never has been. We are social animals who depend on one another for our continued existence. While 'co-dependency' in psychology describes a pathology of mutually assured diminishment, it is just as much a pathology to think that you are 'independent,' or ever will be. Human beings do not exist that way. It is how we engage our dependencies in a healthy way that matters. We live *together!* And if we do not, we do not live well.

Now, Ibn 'Arabi says, "if you know yourself to be without inherent existence … then you may know God." In other words, if we know ourselves to be radically interdependent—extending beyond the borders of our bodies into the air we breathe, into the rivers from which we drink, into the sunlight in which we bask, into the earth from which we grow, into other bodies that we experience, and in which we make new bodies—then we may know ourselves truly! And we may know God.

Putting a nametag on ourselves is like tossing it in a stream and watching it float away!

If I ask you, "How can I find Boulder Creek?"

You may point and say, "Boulder Creek is over there."

The name and the pointing serve a purpose, because I want to get to Boulder Creek, *specifically*, and not Bear Creek. Thus, the name has a meaning and a function for me

So I head in the direction you pointed, and finally I come to a creek. I can see it is a creek, a narrow strip of water with scrub trees growing on either side. "Ah, this is Boulder Creek," I say.

I look left and then right, and I see the creek goes off in

either direction, out beyond my ken, or bends in such a way that I can no longer see where it goes next.

"Wait," I say, "the whole thing is Boulder Creek! This is just a part of it!"

Now, both the pointing in a general direction and the name of my destination, "Boulder Creek," are starting to lose meaning. Reflecting on this, I kneel down and cup some of the water in my hand and ask aloud, "Is this water in my hand Boulder Creek?"

Not anymore. It is but a Heraclitian flux running quickly through my fingers.

Now I say to myself, "Oh, names and forms have a function, but not really a reality beyond the function. The function is practical, but not essential."

If you need me to give an important document to so-and-so, you will tell me their name, identify the place where I can find them, and give me a description of their physical appearance. That description is functional in a specific context. It is not who and what they are; it merely serves a purpose, like a nametag. But, beyond the specific circumstances, it loses meaning. When we get to know the actual person, we see that the description was merely a nametag on a flow phenomenon of interdependence in a vast system of interdependency with no beginning and no end, that we are all part of a great contiguous continuity. Separation is *shirk*.

When God is the "place of the world,"[32] then there is nothing that is not divine, that is not a manifestation of God. Thus, every encounter becomes a divine opportunity, and God the secret meaning, the holy significance buried in every thing, every breath, and every thought.

maqamat

The Stations of the Path

Eleven Traditional Roles in Sufism *

In Arabic music, a *maqam* it is a specific modal structure or melody type; but among Sufis, the word *maqam,* meaning 'place' or 'station,' is a level of sustained integration achieved by an individual initiate, and often marked by a specific role or responsibility in the community.

It is especially common in Sufism to hear a distinction made between *maqamat* and *ahwal*, 'stations' and 'states.' A *hal* (the singular of *ahwal)* is understood to be a temporary 'state,' such as one has in an ecstatic spiritual experience; while a *maqam* is a 'station,' or a 'level' of attainment on the path. As the early Sufi master, Abu'l-Qasim al-Qushayri, put it, states "are gifts; the stations are the earnings."[1] Thus, it is understood in Sufism that while a person may have an illuminating experience in prayer or meditation, this does not necessarily indicate any change in their spiritual identity: it is an experience, not a promotion to the rank of enlightened being.

The *maqam*, however, is more difficult to describe; it is a general state. For instance, a person might conceivably reach a certain level of maturity on the spiritual path, but is still capable of falling into foolishness, or reaching higher. But neither the 'reaching higher' nor the 'falling lower' really has much of an affect on their station in general. It is as if they are standing on a

* An edited version of a talk given in Boulder, Colorado, on March 5th, 2020, at a Thursday night Inayati-Maimuni *Ẕikr* and *Soḥbet*, and earlier talks in Boulder, Colorado, in January of 2017 and 2018, at Naropa University.

wide platform: from that platform or station, they may leap up and feel assured of landing solidly on the platform again; and if they happen to fall down, they are only falling on the platform itself. That is to say, people who have reached a certain level of sustained spiritual integration do fall, but they do not often fall from their station entirely, and tend to get up without too much difficulty. It is their tendency to get up, or the consistency of their getting up, that keeps them at that level.

Qushayri actually describes forty-five distinct 'stations,' in his classic *Risala*, including stations like *tawba* (conversion), *tawakkul* (trust), *zikr* (remembrance), and *shawq* (yearning).[2] Likewise, Hazrat Inayat Khan distinguishes twelve levels of esoteric initiation, including 'testing by the *murshid*,' 'discovering the God-ideal,' and 'expressing the manner of God in one's being.'[3] Paralleling these in number, if not in experiential attainment, are twelve degrees of initiation, acknowledged in some Inayati Sufi lineages, which are essentially ranks associated with capacities to teach different types of material.[4]

Nevertheless, it can be difficult to discern the subtle differences between these 'stations' as integrated qualities, and more temporary 'states' as episodic experiences.[5] Moreover, the path does not usually unfold in a neat linear progression, allowing us to know exactly where we are on that path. Thus, it is best to speak of *maqamat* in terms of specific roles—both experiential and functional—within the holarchy of the *tariqah*, or 'order.'

Because it is not desirable for seekers to be preoccupied with speculations about their own *maqam*, or to identify with one, these roles—usually assigned by the *murshid*—are only seen as a general acknowledgment of apparent maturity on the spiritual path, noting the fulfillment of certain prerequisites, and the taking-up of particular duties and responsibilities related to that *maqam* in the *tariqah*. Though these roles may vary widely in number and type across different Sufi lineages, there are at least eleven relevant stations for Sufis to consider.

The First Maqam—Muhibb

The *muhibb* (f. *muhibba)* is 'one who loves,' or in this case, an 'admirer' of Sufism. The *muhibb* is attracted to the 'fragrance' of Sufism—to its poetry, its music, its *zikr* and *soḥbet*—like a bee drawn to pollen, but has not yet entered the path, formally. It is a station that is associated with what is sometimes called the stage of 'hearing,' where we first encounter the possibility of all that might unfold in us.

The word *muhibb* is also used more specifically for a 'friend of the path,' acknowledging a lateral connection to a particular lineage, even though the person in question is not a *murid* within that lineage. The *muhibb*, in this case, might already be an initiate of a Sufi lineage, but maintains such good relations with another lineage and its adherents, that they are, as it were, almost considered 'part of the family.'

However, when the *muhibb* decides that they want to enter a *tariqah*, a particular Sufi 'path' or lineage, they then enter into the stage or station of the *talib*.

The Second Maqam—Talib

The *talib* (f. *taliba)* is a 'candidate' for entry into the path, one whose desire to walk the Sufi path has led them to seek *bay'ah*, 'initiation.' One may arrive at this decision in a variety of ways: through guidance in a dream, by "falling in love" with the path through a particular *shaykh*, or by simple desire.[6] Of course, the ways of love and dream are preferred over desire. But, however one arrives at the decision, it is an important decision and one not to be taken lightly. Nor is acceptance a foregone conclusion.

A wonderful story is told to Halveti-Jerrahi Sufis at the time of their initiation which illustrates the import of this decision.

There was once a young Sufi *murid,* Ahmet, who had a good friend named Talep. Talep, pleased with what he had heard from Ahmet of the Sufi path, wished to become a Sufi, too. One day, he approached Ahmet and asked him, "Will you speak to your *shaykh* about me?"

Ahmet was overjoyed, and the very next day, approached his master on his friends behalf. *"Effendi,"* he said, "my friend, Talep, who is both honest and hardworking, has asked me to speak to you about joining our circle."

The *shaykh* listened attentively, but said nothing in response; so Ahmet humbly withdrew.

Letting a week or two pass, Ahmet again came back and asked once more. But again, the *shaykh* remained silent.

After a few more weeks, Ahmet asked a third time, and the *shaykh* finally replied, "Let your friend come and serve in the *tekke,* and we'll see if he is ready to join the circle."

Thus, Talep was put to work sweeping and cleaning in the *tekke.* As he worked, he could hear the others practicing *zikr,* talking in *sohbet,* and laughing at meals; but he was not allowed to participate himself.

Seeing him languishing on the margins week-after-week, Ahmet felt sorry for him and approached the *shaykh* once again on Talep's behalf—*"Effendi,* is there perhaps something more Talep might do?"

The *shaykh* replied, "Let him serve me a cup of tea next Thursday during our *sohbet.* If he can serve me successfully, it may be a sign that he is ready to join us."

That Thursday, Talep waited anxiously to be called upon to serve the *shaykh.* When the time came, the master signaled for the tea, and Talep rushed forward with a cup of tea on a tray and quickly knelt before the *shaykh.* The *shaykh,* who was then in the middle of a story, gestured to make a point just as Talep reached out with the tea, accidentally knocking the cup from his hand and spilling it all over the floor! Talep was horrified and quickly shut his eyes!

When he opened them, he found himself teetering on the edge of a mountain with a forest behind him. Disoriented, he was not sure what had happened, but he looked around and decided he had better make his way down the mountain. He walked down through the mountain forest until he came to a town where he smelled a wonderful aroma coming from a nearby restaurant. Although he knew he had not any money, he took a seat in the restaurant anyway and ordered a meal. After dessert and coffee, a well-dressed man came to the table and asked him if he had enjoyed his meal. Talep said, "Yes, everything was wonderful. Are you the owner?"

"Yes," the man replied. "I am so glad you enjoyed the meal."

Talep then made as if to look for his money (though he knew he had none) and exclaimed suddenly, "Oh! I must have lost my money somewhere! How can I pay you back?"

The owner shook his head, gesturing for him to stop. "You must not be from around here, friend. You are my guest. No payment is required. But I would ask your blessing on my house and my family."

So Talep made an eloquent blessing and left.

Feeling full and content, he went for a stroll to enjoy the late afternoon air. He passed a tailor's shop and stopped to admire a beautifully embroidered vest in the shop window. As he gazed at the vest, the owner of the shop came out and said, "Do you like that vest?"

"Yes," said the young man. "The embroidery is very beautiful."

"Then it's yours," said the owner. "It looks just your size!"

Talep told the tailor that he had no money, but the tailor insisted it was a gift! Then the tailor said, "You're not from around here, are you? Perhaps you're needing a place to stay? . . . Do me a favor; I have a room above the shop, and it would be good to have someone staying in it and keeping an eye on the shop for me at night. Is it a deal?"

In this way, Talep suddenly found himself, all in one day, well-fed in a new vest and cozy in his own room, free from rent. Having all of his needs taken care of in an almost miraculous fashion, he lay down upon the bed thinking he must be in paradise.

At just that moment, he heard the lovely sound of many women's voices outside his window. So he went to the window and saw that the plaza below was indeed filled with women socializing. Amazingly, he saw that it was *only* women; there were no men in the plaza at all! And there among the women was the most beautiful young woman he had ever seen.

That night, he could not sleep for the vision of the young woman in his mind. So the next morning, he approached the tailor and asked about the women gathering in the plaza. The tailor said, "Oh, Thursday night is *'ladies' night,'* when the women of the town gather together outside and all the men stay in."

The tailor looked at Talep and asked with a smile, "Did you perhaps see a particularly lovely woman?" Talep smiled and the tailor said, "Many a man has seen his future wife for the first time at such gatherings. When this happens, he carries a lighted candle into the host of women the next Thursday and gives it to the woman he wishes to marry. If she accepts it from him, she has accepted his proposal of marriage."

The following Thursday, Talep carried a lighted candle into the crowd and offered it to the beautiful young woman he had seen the week before. She looked at him a moment and then accepted the candle with a modest smile. Not knowing what else to do, Talep stood there awkwardly a few seconds before turning around and hurrying back to his little room.

The next morning, he was awakened by loud and heavy knocks upon his door! He soon found himself facing two large soldiers. His stomach lurched. Had the tailor perhaps played a trick on him? Terrified, he asked, "What have I done?"

"You're to come with us; you've been summoned to the office of the town's chief magistrate."

Moments later, he found himself before a stern-looking magistrate whose gaze seemed to pierce him. But to his surprise, the magistrate said, "It seems my daughter has accepted your proposal. Her dowry includes a house and enough money for servants and for you to make investments to support her. However, before you marry my daughter, you must make me three promises."

Talep was so eager to marry the beautiful young woman that he would have promised anything. "Of course," he said. "What are your conditions?"

The magistrate said, "You must guard well your tongue, your hands, and your sex. Do you promise?"

"I do!" said the eager young man.

So the couple was married and Talep thought himself the luckiest man in the world.

One morning, sometime later, as the young husband and his new bride slept late, there was a knock at the door. Suddenly, Talep remembered that he had made an appointment with some men to talk about an investment. Not wanting to be bothered at that moment, he said to his wife, "My wife, those are some men with whom I had an appointment. Will you please tell them that I have already gone out and will meet with them later this afternoon?"

Surprised, his wife asked, "What do you want me to tell them!?"

Somewhat impatiently, Talep said, "Tell them I have gone out and will see them this afternoon!"

Noticeably upset, his wife quickly dressed and left the room. After she did not come back as expected, he got up to look for her. She was not in the house! Talep then had the sinking feeling that he might find her at her father's house.

When he arrived, his father-in-law, the magistrate, greeted him angrily, saying, "Already you have failed to keep your first promise! Worse, not only have you failed to guard your own tongue, you have asked my daughter and your wife to lie for you, too!"

Talep begged forgiveness and promised it would never happen again and soon everything was back to normal.

A few weeks later, Talep and his wife went out for a picnic in the countryside. As his wife rested on a blanket, he went for a little walk. Passing an orchard, he came face-to-face with a low-hanging branch with a perfect peach upon it. As it was hanging over the orchard's fence and so ripe that it was clearly about to fall from the branch, he decided he might as well pick it before it falls to the ground and is wasted. He picked the peach and took it back to his wife and asked her to cut it up for dessert.

His young bride asked, "Where did you get this? Did you buy it? Did someone give it to you?"

"No," Talep answered. "It was just about to fall from the branch of a tree hanging over the fence of an orchard. It would have been wasted if I had left it."

His young bride's face fell when she heard this, and again she ran off, this time in tears. When he could not find her, he knew he must go to the house of his father-in-law, the magistrate, to look for her. The magistrate upbraided him once more: "This is the second promise you have broken! You promised to guard your hands! That peach was not yours: it had not fallen; you did not buy it; and no one had given it to you as a gift!"

Again, the young husband begged forgiveness and was reluctantly—*very reluctantly*—given another chance to prove himself worthy of his bride.

Months passed, and one day Talep found himself walking by the river on a Tuesday, the day the women took their laundry to the river to wash. Actually, it may not have been wholly accidental, as he always enjoyed seeing the many lovely women at their washing. Talep knew his wife was beautiful, of course, but he had become accustomed to her looks and noticed her less and less. Thus, he began to walk by the river every Tuesday, watching the women longer and longer each week. Finally, one week he stopped and concealed himself behind a great boulder so that he could watch them freely, without anyone else noticing. But just then, he was grabbed from behind by two huge soldiers who knew exactly what he was doing!

The soldiers brought Talep before his father-in-law, the magistrate, and reported on what they had seen. The magistrate had heard enough. He stared coldly at his son-in-law and said: "You have broken your third promise. Though you have not yet had the opportunity to act out your desires, you have shown that you would do so if given the opportunity. Your behavior shows you are not worthy of my daughter." He then turned to the soldiers and said, "Take him back to where he came from!"

So the soldiers marched Talep back up the mountain, through the forest, to the cliff's edge from which he had come. Suddenly, he realized what was about to happen; but it was too late. They threw him over! In terror, Talep, hurtling toward the rocks below, closed his eyes . . . *and heard the sound of breaking glass!*

Talep opened his eyes and found himself kneeling in front of the *shaykh*, still holding the tray and looking down at the broken and spilled cup of tea.

Talep was confused and disoriented.

Then the *shaykh* leaned forward and whispered gently in his ear, "You see, you are not yet ready."[7]

It is a story full of symbolic significance. Entering the Sufi path, one finds oneself overwhelmed by gifts and generosity, a characteristic of a Sufi circle. It is a family, and in that family, you will be taken care of. Thursday night is indeed "ladies' night," the night of Sufi practice, when you meet the 'bride,' the feminine presence of God. The chief magistrate, of course, is the *shaykh,* with whom you make an 'oath,' *bay'ah*—"guard well your tongue, your hands, and your sex."[8] And, as we see, the understanding of these promises is not the common understanding, but presupposes a higher level of responsibility. In the end, the *talib* falls short of his responsibilities, and falls hard!

It can be a discouraging story. But note that it is not told in the Halveti-Jerrahi lineage to 'candidates' for initiation, but to new initiates! Which suggests that it is only meant to be a cautionary tale, a reminder of just how easy it is to take the gifts of the path for granted while failing in our responsibilities to it.

But it also illustrates the essential characteristic of the *talib*'s station, the period of discernment. In many Turkish Sufi orders, it was the custom for the *talib* to undergo a forty-day 'ordeal' of solitary contemplation, called a *chilla.* If the *talib* was young, they would have to get their parents' permission first. In order to qualify for the *chilla,* they would enter the *tekke,* meaning 'place of refuge,' for a three-day trial, kneeling on an animal hide outside the *chilla'khana,* 'place of ordeal,' with head bowed. In this context, the *talib* was called an *'iqrar,* a 'pledge' or 'promise.' They were not allowed to leave the animal hide except to relieve themselves, or by the permission of the *shaykh* to perform a specific task.[9]

The task was usually designed as a test to gauge the *'iqrar'*s patience, virtue, and reliability. Dhun-Nun al-Misri of Egypt once gave a *talib* the task of taking a box to a companion in a distant village, saying, "Under no circumstances are you to open the box." But, somewhere along the way, overcome by boredom or curiosity on the long journey, the disciple opened the box. Out jumped a mouse which quickly escaped! When the young man returned from his unsuccessful mission, Dhun-Nun said to him, "We entrusted you with a mouse, and you betrayed him; how do you expect us to entrust you with divine secrets? Be on your way."[10]

If the 'pledge' was unable to complete the trial, or the *chilla* that followed, they were not easily admitted to another trial.[11]

However, tasks could also be much simpler, such as sweeping the floors in the *tekke*, or helping out with various needs in the community, or serving the *shaykh* in some way. This allowed the community to take the measure of the *talib*'s commitment, watching how the *talib* worked, noticing whether they were diligent and fastidious in their tasks. It also tested the *talib*'s patience and commitment over a series of weeks or months, and allowed them to discern for themselves whether they really wanted such a life.

How does the *shaykh* discern whether the *talib* should be initiated? Sometimes just by intuition and shrewd observation. They observe the character and qualities of the *talib* in their service, judging whether they belong in the particular circle. Other times, the *shaykh* will ask for guidance from a dream offering indications or counter-indications as to whether the *talib* should be initiated.[12] The dream will also sometimes give information in symbolic form that speaks to the individual's particular path.

Acceptance of the *talib* might also be much simpler. According to Shaykh Abdul Aziz Said (b. ca.1930), when potential murids would come to Shaykh Ahmed, the great Syrian Qadiri-Rufai master, there would be clotheslines strung with wet sheets hanging. If a prospective *murid,* without prompting or being told ahead of time, would feel the sheets for dryness, and finding a sheet dry, take it down and fold it, that person was accepted as Shaykh Ahmed's *murid.*[13]

When a *talib* is refused, it is often on the basis of internal guidance, whether from a dream, or the *shaykh*'s refined relationship to their own intuition. My own *murshid* would sometimes respond to an aspirant, "I'm sorry; I don't have the root of your soul." He believed that deep connections pre-exist a relationship that make those relationships obvious when they arise, and he seemed to know when those connections were not present. There might be some affinity, but not the relationship of teacher and student. "You are connected 'at the root' somewhere else," he would say. If they were fortunate, he might have an idea where. But if the *talib* is accepted and offered initiation, they are considered ready to start on the endless path.

The Third Maqam—Murid

The *murid* (f. *murida)*, or 'seeker,' is an initiate in a Sufi lineage.

The *talib* who becomes truly receptive to guidance, and who is accepted by a *shaykh,* is recognized as a *murid* through *bay'ah,* 'initiation.' The Arabic word, *bay'ah,* literally refers to a 'deal' or 'agreement,' formally sealed by the striking together of hands. In the time of the prophet Muḥammad, peace and blessings be upon him, the *bay'ah* and its handshake were part of an oath of allegiance, which later became the basis of the Sufi practice of 'taking hand' with a *shaykh.*

Initiation rituals vary from order-to-order and lineage-to-lineage. In the medieval period, in the Chishti *tariqah,* the prospective initiate would be expected to fast the day of the initiation. They would then take the hand of the *shaykh* while affirming a formal oath. When this was accomplished, their hair would be cut and they might receive a *tesbiḥ* (prayer beads) and *khirqa* (cloak, lit. 'rag') from the *shaykh.* They would then perform two cycles of ritual prayer and bow formally before the *shaykh,* to whom they would offer a gift. Gifts might also be offered to their fellow murids, and to the wider community as charity.[14]

Nevertheless, the oath and the taking of the hand are the core elements. Among Chishtis of that time, if the master and disciple were of different genders, then the symbolic act of 'taking hand' was replaced with another symbolic act. A bowl of water would be brought forth and the initiate would put a hand in, followed by the master, who would then administer the oath of the Chishtiyya . . .

> You have sworn an oath *('ahd)* with this broken one, and with the master of this broken one, with the masters of Chisht, with the followers of the followers, with the followers [of the Prophet], with the Messenger of the Lord of Creation, with the bearers of the Canopy,[15] and with God Himself. Guard your eye, and guard your tongue. Do not speak evil of anyone nor think evil of anyone. Do not bring harm to anyone, and do not approach forbidden things. Remain on the path of the religious law *(shar').* You have sworn an oath to all of this, so observe these conditions.[16]

However, not all initiatory rites are so formal, or so conventional. An interesting story was told to me by Michael Kosacoff, an initiate of Shaykh Abdul Aziz Said. Feeling some caution about initiation, Kosacoff, a native New Yorker said boldly: "You're a Rufai! I know about you; you're the ones who take a Damascus steel blade and pierce the flesh of a *murid!* I don't believe in the desecration of the flesh."

To which, Shaykh Abdul Aziz, sitting at his desk in his office at American University, responded, "I won't do that to you." He then reached into his drawer and took out a ring.

"I don't wear rings," said Kosacoff.

"Put it on a necklace around your neck then."

"I don't wear jewelry."

"Then put it in your pocket."

Kosacoff took the ring and put it in his pocket.

Within a week, he was wearing the ring. "I did not *want* to wear the ring," he told me, "but the ring *commanded* it!" And he found that after he started to wear the ring, his heart opened more and more, and he began to pray. But he soon noticed that when his heart was closed, the ring began to cut his finger! He then took the ring off and found that it was actually sharp! He had not noticed this before.

He then went to see Shaykh Abdul Aziz, who immediately pointed at the ring on his finger and smiled, almost laughing, as if to say, *I thought you didn't wear jewelry?!*[17]

Rufai Sufis have old traditions concerning such practices. Traditionally, if a Rufai Sufi was lost in an authentic *wajd,* or 'ecstatic experience,' they could be pierced by metal skewers without any blood or harm to the body. Here we have a Rufai *murid* resisting this tradition and finding that the pattern of this peculiar initiatory rite managed to accomplish itself despite his best efforts to avoid it!

This is an aspect of spiritual life with which the *murid* must come to terms: the path leads us where it wills and has its own desires for us. That is to say, the *murid* has entered into a path with its own energetic patterns which now become operative in their life, and with which they must contend, or to which they must ultimately surrender.

The specific work and duties of the *murid,* however, are outlined in numerous places across the tradition. One succinct description is given by the Nuriyya-Malamiyya *shaykh,* Mehmet Selim Öziç (1930-2018), and his primary successor, Yannis Toussulis . . .

> The commitment of the *murid* is to progress beyond the stage of the "commanding *nafs,*" encounter and overcome the "blaming *nafs.*" The specific qualities of which include: blaming others, backbiting, trickery and conceitedness. After taking formal initiation *(bay'at haqiqa),* the *murid* must form a strong internal bond *(rabita)* with the guide, follow the latter's instructions diligently, soften and open the heart, undergo tests of loyalty, continue to question with utter politeness and sincerity, and (above all) fan the flame of inspiration or of ardent devotion *('ishq)* to God.[18]

That is to say, the *murid* is one who, having formed a deep spiritual connection *(rabita)* with a *shaykh,* receives guidance from them, learning to overcome the *nafs al-ammara*, the tyrannical aspects of the ego, and to address the claims of the *nafs al-lawwama,* the regretful self, doing what one can to make up for past and present wrongs.

Although the *murid* may advance to other *maqamat* in time, from another perspective, a *murid* is always a *murid,* seeking God in love.

The Fourth Maqam—Salik

The *salik* (f. *salika)* is a 'traveler.'

Among the primary metaphors of the Sufi path is 'traveling,' taking a journey. It was also a literal expectation;

Sufis were expected to travel in search of guidance. Walking is a contemplative exercise, naturally cultivating contemplation, from which guidance arises. Often, the *shaykh* would send a *murid* to another *shaykh* in a distant region to learn a particular lesson, a practice or a teaching. But they were also to learn from the traveling itself, to learn what traveling had to teach them about a 'path,' about the twists and turns of a journey. Traveling a road with a staff, a flagon of water, and a *kashkul* or 'begging bowl,' doing *zikr,* as they walked, they learned the lesson of reliance on God, *tawakkul.*[19]

In this sense, all Sufis are *salikun,* 'travelers,' making *suluk,* the great 'journey.'

The *maqam* of the *salik,* however, refers to a Sufi *murid* who now 'knows the ropes.' If a new *murid* should enter the circle, they can tell them where to sit, or the basic etiquette of any given situation. They know the fundamentals of the Sufi circle, the basic practices and teachings, and can also represent them in a basic way. Thus, they are the primary 'servitors' of the community, or *akhdam.*

From the moment a person becomes a *murid* (even from the moment they become a *talib)* they begin service. The *khadim,* or 'servitor,' serves the Sufi community, specifically in social situations, at *zikr* and *soḥbet,* or in the *khanegah,* the Sufi 'traveler's house.' They arrange the space; they see to the needs of the participants; they serve the food and drinks, 'considering the circle.'[20] They even serve in the kitchen.

The kitchen is considered a place of training, for 'cooking' is another of the great metaphors for the Sufi path. We all start the path as 'uncooked food,' raw and immature, unpalatable. It is God and the path that 'cook' us, making us mature and something healthy for the diet of the planet.[21] So *salikun* serve in the kitchen to see what it means to have a good clean workspace, what ingredients are necessary, what tools are necessary, how to boil the water and chop the vegetables, to learn how different meals are assembled, how they are cooked with precision and plated to eat.

The *salik* is firm in the path, resolved and determined to refrain from ignorant behaviors and harming others.

The Fifth Maqam—Faqir-Darvish

The *faqir* (f. *faqirah)* is 'one who is poor,' or a 'beggar,' and the *darvish* is 'one who stands on the threshold,' like a beggar.[22] *Faqir* and *darvish* are common synonyms for Sufis in general. The references to 'poverty' and 'begging' are historically connected to early Sufis leading ascetic lifestyles, often on the road as *salikun,* 'travelers,' carrying a *kashkul,* or 'begging bowl.' However, it is also symbolic of a realization that everything we have comes from God. We are just like beggars; and if we have the ability to give, it is because we first received.[23]

This *maqam* is the goal of the Sufi path. The goal is not to become a Sufi *shaykh.* That is a vocation. Sufis might have various vocations—being painters, doctors, waitors, musicians, tailors, writers, gardeners, accountants, lawyers, or cooks—and all of these might come to be *fuqara'* or *daravish,* good 'faqirs' or 'dervishes,' reliant on God. For that is the real goal of the path—to become spiritually mature individuals integrated in society, not shaykhs.

Sufism, by its very nature, is a subversive tradition: it undermines the pathological elements of common culture; for when it is actualized, it sends mature individuals back into society, to walk among others, to work in banks and teach Yoga, to be police officers and schoolteachers, planted like 'sleeper agents' in the world. Because this is where we need holiness . . . in the world, not outside of it.

The attributes of the *faqir* or *darvish* are "generosity, contentment, modesty, liberality, and gratitude," as well as "dignity, sincerity, courage, compassion, and complete loyalty."[24]

The *faqir or darvish* has integrated and exemplifies those things that the *salik* only knows by education. Like the *salik*, the *faqir* or *darvish* is also a *khadim*, a 'servant' to other Sufis; but their service is now completely natural, the results from deep training, and extends beyond the *halqah*, the Sufi 'circle,' to the world. They are exemplary Sufis in the world, and models of practice, humility, learning, and service, for the *talibun, muridun,* and *salikun* of the *tariqah.*

The Sixth Maqam—Chiragh

The term, *chiragh* (f. *chiraghah)*, 'candle' or 'light,' is mostly used among Inayati Sufis for a ritual functionary.[25] In the Inayati-Maimuni lineage, it is used more generally. This is, *ideally*, a mature Sufi, already a *faqir* or *darvish*, with a clearly discernable vocation, entrusted with mentoring in the *halqah* according to that vocation. This would parallel the function of 'babas' among some Bektashi lineages, mentors "with skills to pass on, such as sewing, dancing, music and so on." The *baba* also acted as an elder mentor in Sufi practices, and helped guide newer murids through retreats.[26] But many traditional roles in a Sufi 'traveler's house' *(khanegah)* fit this *maqam*, such as 'tea-master,' 'keeper of the cauldron,' 'keeper of the lamps,' etc.

The founder of the Inayati lineage, Hazrat Inayat Khan, established "Five Activities" under which most of these *chiragh* functions would fall. Those who had trained and achieved mastery in a given vocation would serve as mentors and leaders in one of these "Activities."

> *Tariqah*. The first activity is the inner 'path' *(tariqah)*, studying the teachings and training in the practices of classical Sufism *(tasawwuf)* and universalist Sufism, as taught by Hazrat Inayat Khan. Among different lineages of Inayati Sufism, this is sometimes called the "Inner School" or the "Esoteric School."

Shafa'. The second activity is 'healing' *(shafa')* or 'interceding' *(shafa'a),* comprised of the esoteric teachings and practices of Hazrat Inayat Khan regarding the physical, psychological, and spiritual health and well-being of the individual.

Qabilah. The third activity is 'tribe' *(qabilah)* or 'family' *(usrah),* dealing with the health and well-being of the individual in society and society as a whole, especially as expressed in the Rules of Hazrat Inayat Khan. Among different lineages of Inayati Sufism, this is sometimes called "Kinship."

Zira'a. The fourth activity is ecology or 'cultivation' *(zira'a),* dealing with the welfare of the planet, focusing on the esoteric teachings of Hazrat Inayat Khan on ecological stewardship. Among different lineages of Inayati Sufism, this is sometimes called "Zirat."

'Ibadah. The fifth activity is 'worship' *(ibadah),* dealing with the trans-confessional teachings and worship service of Hazrat Inayat Khan, honoring the major religious traditions, with its own prayers, rituals, and teachings. Among the lineages of Inayati Sufism, this is generally called, "Universal Worship."

The Seventh Maqam—Khalifa

The *khalifa,* meaning 'deputy' or 'steward,' is a successor and representative of the *shaykh* or *murshid,* formally apprenticing in the art of spiritual guidance within the *tariqah.* Having been selected for special training by the *shaykh* (to become a *shaykh),* seeming to have that vocation, the *khalifa* is expected to push the limits of spiritual work and study,[27] pursuing mastery.

Within the *halqah,* or the *khanegah,* the *khalifa* functions as the *shaykh*'s mouthpiece with regard to practical affairs, especially at gatherings. The *khalifa* is also often cast in the role of 'admonisher.' Where the *shaykh* is loving and accepting, the *khalifa* will be directed to reprove the same person . . . 'Get it together! How could you have let the mouse out of the box!' This gentle reproof or admonishment is called *tanbih,* literally, an 'awakening.' But neither the *shaykh* or the *khalifa* is being disingenuous. A person often needs both messages: they need to be loved unconditionally, and challenged to grow. This is done intentionally through these two roles. Thus, it is accepted in the *halqah* that the reproof of the *khalifa* is as necessary as the consoling of the *shaykh.*[28]

My own *murshid* sent me on a number of occasions with 'bad news' for somebody else, which was difficult for me, because I definitely did not want to be the person to deliver that news, or to figure out how to tell them that he had said, "No." But if I was to be a *shaykh,* I had to learn to do it, because it is a responsibility. It was hard for the hearer, hard for me, and thus, maturing for us both.

As with the *shaykh* and *murid (piri-muridi)* relationship, a *khalifa* is always spoken of as a *khalifa,* or representative of a particular *shaykh,* even after they become a *shaykh* themselves. They are the elder *shaykh*'s representative wherever they may go, wherever they may serve.

Though one *khalifa* may be primary, it is not uncommon for a *shaykh* to have many *khulafa',* 'deputies.' Indeed, when Khwaja Nizam ad-Din 'Awliyya was in his last illness, a list of thirty possible successors was drawn up.[29] Again, it is a matter of vocation and qualification and varies from *shaykh* to *shaykh.*

The Eighth Maqam—Shaykh-Murshid

The *shaykh* (f. *shaykha)* is an 'elder,' and the *murshid* (f. *murshida)* a 'guide.' The word *shaykh* was originally used in pre-Islamic Arabia for a tribal leader, and gradually came into use in Sufism for a 'master,' probably in the sense of being a 'respected elder' considered wise. Though *murshid,* 'guide' might be more accurate to the *maqam.*

The *shaykh* or *murshid,* in Sufi terms, is a *sajjada-nishin,* 'one who sits on the carpet' or prayer rug of their predecessor, becoming the new *shaykh as-sajjada,* 'elder of the carpet,' the "'throne' of the order," as it were, overseeing ceremonies of initiation and investiture.[30]

A *khalifa'* may become a *shaykh* by election, by inheritance, or by investiture and authorization within the previous *shaykh*'s lifetime.

Before the Halveti-Jerrahi *shaykh,* Fahreddin Effendi passed in 1966, he had named his *khalifa,* my own murshid's friend, Muzaffer Ozak, his successor as head of the lineage.[31] Even so, some of the senior dervishes objected. So they met in conclave to vote on the matter. But to everyone's surprise, the senior dervish who had been most opposed to Muzaffer Effendi, perhaps thinking himself most qualified, had changed his mind, saying, "I am now convinced that you are to be our *shaykh,* and I wish to be the first to kiss your hand as such." When asked about his change of heart, he told them . . .

> "I have changed my opinion because of a dream I had last night," he explained. "I dreamed that I was leading the dervishes in the ceremony of Remembrance of God, but nothing went right. There was no unity in the chanting or in the movement of the dervishes. Then Muzaffer [Effendi] led the ceremony and everything went perfectly smoothly."[32]

Hearing this, the rest of the dissenters came around and Muzaffer Effendi was unanimously elected *shaykh.*

Within the previous *shaykh*'s lifetime, the authorization and investiture of a new *shaykh* is often literal and formal. After discussing his own imminent death, Khwaja Mu'in ad-Din

Chishti made Khwaja Qutb ad-Din his successor, as described by the latter in *Dalil al-'Arifin* . . .

> "Later the Shaykh ordered 'Ali Sanjari: 'Write a document indicating that Qutb ad-Din should go to Delhi since we have given him the authority to succeed us and Delhi should be his place of work.' When the document was completed, it was given into the hand of this well-wisher. I fell face down on the ground, and the Shaykh said, 'Draw nearer.' I came closer to him. He placed a turban and a cap on the head of this *faqir*, and the staff of Khwaja 'Usman Harwani in my hand, and the patched cloak *[khirqa]* on my back. He also gave me the Holy Qur'an, the prayer carpet, and the wooden shoes. 'This is a trust from the Prophet,' he noted, 'which has been handed down by my master (i.e., the pre-Indian Chishti *shaykhs*). I bequeath it to you so that on the Day of Judgment I will not have to hide my face in shame before those saints who preceded me.' I prostrated myself and said two rounds of prayer. The Khwaja took my hand and, looking to heaven, declared: 'Go, I entrust you to God, and I will see you safely to your goal.' [...]
>
> "Then I went to Delhi and settled there."[33]

This is a literal *investiture*, meaning 'to clothe' or 'adorn,' especially with articles that belong to the *shaykh*, or which belonged to previous *shuyukh* in the lineage. At my own investiture, after a private ceremony, my *murshid* called a witness and removed his green cloak and turban and placed them on me as a symbol of succession. And after his passing, these garments and many other items came to me as an inheritance.

But a formal authorization is also mentioned in Khwaja Qutb ad-Din's account. This is known as a *khilafat-nama* or *ijazah-nama*, a 'letter of succession' or 'authorization.' The simplest *ijazah* might do little more than establish the genealogies of transmission of the 'masters in chain,' the *silsila* of the *shaykh,* and certify the passing of that transmission.[34] But others might add practices and admonitions . . .

> 1. to purify the resolution for bestowing *irshad* (guidance); 2. to know their own capacity, as well of that of the *murid* (seeker); 3. to be pure with respect to the murid's property; 4. to always make offerings from their own welfare; 5. to make an accord of thought, word, and deed in their own practice, setting the example for the *murid;* 6. to have compassion for weakness and frailty in others; 7. to purify their speech of desire; 8. to make the heart transparent to God when speaking; 9. to speak ambiguously of the faults of others, gently, and in disguise; 10. to preserve the mysteries of the *murid;* 11. to pardon the mistakes of the *murid;* 12. to pass over their own rights; 13. to allow the rights of the *murid;* 14. to take time for their own *khilvat* (retreat); and 15. to increase the practice of *nawafil* (practicing beyond the norm).[35]

This is interesting because it names the responsibilities of what it is to be a *shaykh,* not the responsibilities of others to the *shaykh.* This is what so often is turned around in the pathological spirituality of guru veneration.

The Ninth Maqam—Murad

The *murad* is the 'one sought,' or 'destination.' Although this title is often used synonymously with *shaykh* or *murshid,* it is here used to designate a *murshid's murshid.* It is a *maqam* of respect for those who came before us, and a reminder to all that the teacher also has a teacher. We are all 'in chain.' If you look to the *shaykh* or *murshid,* you should know that they are also looking to another, the *murad*. The practice of *fana' fi-shaykh*, 'making one's self transparent and open to the *shaykh*,' is not a closed process, ending with one opaque spiritual master. It is actually a chain of transparency, as the *shaykh* 'above' is *fana' fi-shaykh* to another, allowing *all* to be seen according to Truth, and not mere appearances.

The Tenth Maqam—Pir-o-Murshid

The *pir-o-murshid* (f. *pirni/pirain-o-murshida)* is the 'elder and guide.' In many Sufi lineages, *pir, murad, murshid,* and *shaykh,* are all used synonymously. However, in the Inayati lineages, springing from the transmission of Hazrat Pir-o-Murshid Inayat Khan, the title *pir,* or more formally *pir-o-murshid,* is reserved for the head of an Inayati lineage. (Interestingly, in traditional environments, the pir's wife is honored as the *pirani,* and his mother, the *pir-ma.)*[36]

The *pir* is the 'keeper' or 'guardian of the lineage,' holding its traditions as a sacred trust, and transmitting them with care to future generations. Above the *pir* is the "Seal of the Saints," the *qutb.*[37]

The Eleventh Maqam—Qutb

The word *qutb* means 'pole,' or 'axis.' The idea of the *qutb* in Sufism is that there is always, somewhere on the planet, a person who is the 'fulcrum' or 'axis' of events, a person by whose actions all of humanity is judged. The *qutb* or *ghauth,* 'help,' embodies the best qualities of humanity, often in the worst circumstances. Depending on their actions in these circumstances, we are judged worthy of survival, of continuing as a species, or not.[38] From this perspective, Jesus—through his agony in the garden, his trials before the judges, his scourging and crucifixion—might very well have been the *qutb,* maintaining the best of what it is to be human, being profoundly loving and compassionate, even as the worst was being done to him without cause.

A person might be the *qutb* for a lifetime, for a decade, for a year, a week, a day, or even a single moment before the role passes to another. According to my *murshid,* Zalman Sulayman, his friend Pir Vilayat Inayat Khan, the son of Hazrat Inayat Khan, believed the *qutb* was, at some point from the mid-1970s to the 1980s, living and at work in Lebanon, perhaps during its protracted civil war.[39] For, according to the early Sufi master, Abu'l-Hasan Hujwiri, the *qutb* must give their attention to 'weak spots' on the planet.[40]

Some people even claim to have met the *qutb*. Abu Bakr Warraq of Tirmidh (d. 893), tells of how Muḥammad ibn Ali al-Hakim once led him on a mysterious journey . . .

> One day Muḥammad b. Ali (al-Hakim) said that he would take me somewhere. I replied: 'It is for the Shaykh to command.' Soon after we set out I saw an exceedingly dreadful wilderness, and in the midst thereof a golden throne placed under a green tree beside a fountain of running water. Seated on the throne was a person clad in beautiful raiment, who rose when Muḥammad b. Ali approached, and bid him sit on the throne. After a while, people came from every side until forty were gathered together. Then Muḥammad b. Ali waived his hand, and immediately food appeared from heaven, and we ate. Afterwards, Muḥammad b. Ali asked a question of a man who was present, and he in reply made a long discourse of which I did not understand a single word. At last the Shaykh begged leave and took his departure, saying to me, 'Go, for thou art blest.' On our return to Tirmidh, I asked him what was that place and who was that man. He told me that the place was the Desert of the Israelites *(tih-i Bani Isra'il)* and that the man was the *Qutb* on whom the order of the universe depends."[41]

The forty who gathered with them there were likely the *abdal*, a group of saints who support the *qutb* around the world, doing the large and small things, mostly unnoticed, that keep the world turning.[42]

What is the spiritual value of this idea if we cannot know who the *qutb* might be at any given moment? Perhaps that itself is its value: it may be anyone of us, at any moment.[43] The *qutb* is the ideal of human possibility. It is the notion of rising to meet the moment of necessity, of being our best in the worst of circumstances. It is understandable for a person to collapse under the pressure of certain conditions. But when we rise up to meet those circumstances with dignity, holding all that potential together for even a moment, we also hold the possibility of changing the world.[44]

baking

Sufism and the Inner Life

An Interview with Pir Netanel Mu'in ad-Din Miles-Yépez *

Question: What draws you to the spiritual path?

Pir Netanel: I think it is a question about *'wholeness'* that draws me to the spiritual path. I ask myself—'Am I whole? How can I become whole?' We all know there are limits—that we have limitations with which we learn to live—but where are they, really? I want to know—Where are my real limits? And have I tested them sufficiently?

Through a good part of my life, I was plagued by debilitating fears and anxieties that limited my freedom and caused me problems. But I finally reached a point where I hated the fears and limitations more than the things that made me afraid and anxious in the first place. I wondered what lay beyond the limits I had set for myself with these fears. How much more of the circle of my life could I occupy if I stopped giving-in to my fears?

In a sense, wholeness is the ultimate reality for me, what in Jungian terms might be called the 'Self.' Wholeness is what I am seeking, not 'Enlightenment.' That has become

---

* An edited version of an interview originally conducted in Boulder, Colorado, on June 20th, 2015, for the Season of the Rose, the annual summer school of the Inayati Order, in New Lebanon, New York, at the Abode of the Message, June 26th to July 1st, 2015. The questions were formulated by Murshid Gayan Macher, a senior teacher in the Inayati Order, in preparation for a public dialogue on "The Inner Life in Inayati Sufism."

the ultimate spiritual ego-trap. I like what Pir Vilayat Inayat Khan used to say on the subject—"Enlightenment is a receding wave." As we walk out into the ocean of consciousness, the wave of enlightenment is always moving on, out beyond us! In that sense, there is only 'enlighten-*ing,*' not 'enlighten-*ment.*'[1] 'Enlighten-ment' is something static, but 'enlighten-ing' is something occurring continuously on the path to wholeness.

Question: And how is that process going so far?

Pir Netanel: Well, from one perspective—looking at the kind of difficulties we all go through—I could say, 'Not very well at this particular moment.' But, from another perspective—looking at where I was twenty years ago—I see that there has clearly been some kind of progress. There are different versions of me along that timeline that were seriously affected by fears and limitations that do not affect me so much now. Maybe that is just maturation.

Question: What do you most admire in a human being? What qualities and ways of being?

Pir Netanel: I admire courage, kindness, sincerity, humility, and hard work in a person.

Question: Does one need to be on a formal spiritual path to become that kind of person?

Pir Netanel: No . . . People make a thousand decisions every day that either divorce them from those qualities or cultivate them; and they make them for a thousand different reasons. They don't necessarily do it because they are on a formal spiritual path, unless we call the desire to cultivate those qualities a "spiritual path." The desire, the decision, and the action are what are important. They are the basic ingredients found in all the formal spiritual paths. What the spiritual path offers is an enhanced set of tools for cultivating those qualities, and for navigating the difficulties that arise in life.

Question: There are many authentic spiritual paths and realized teachers available to us in the world today; are they all basically the same?

Pir Netanel: I want to play devil's advocate for a moment and ask—Are there really so many realized teachers? What do we really know about "authentic spiritual paths" and "realized teachers"? I am not sure I know what that means. Nor am I sure we can afford to believe that as a starting point. All we can do is watch and learn, apply and test.

I hope I am on an authentic path, but I cannot 'sell you' on its authenticity. I can only try to be authentic in it. That is the best any of us can do. If I am in any measure "authentic" in practicing it, and its benefits seem apparent to others, then that might be enough to convince them to give it a try. But does that make it authentic? For all they know, maybe I am just a good fake. The only authenticity for which we can really be responsible is our own, and even that is not necessarily "authenticity." We can try to be sincere, and that's it. We are authentic only to the degree that we are sincere, and that authenticity only relates to the sincerity itself, not necessarily to what is being done sincerely.

As to "realized," we have to ask—'What have they realized?' If, as a so-called 'spiritual teacher,' I am supposed to be 'a realized being' in the way that phrase is usually bandied-about, then I have to say, *I'm not.* Not as some sort of permanent identity, or paragon of idealized virtues, transcending the vicissitudes of life in the world. I am not that; nor do I find that particularly desirable. Have I realized 'something'? Sure. But so has everyone else. The question is—Have I realized something *you* want to know, and can I convey that information to you? Or rather, can I be helpful in helping you to realize it yourself? That is the functional definition of a spiritual teacher. There is no need to make an idol out of the person. Indeed, we *must not* make an idol out of them if we would obtain any real benefit from the spiritual path.

Given all this, I don't think we can know whether all authentic spiritual paths and realized teachers are the same, any more than we can say they are authentic or realized.

Question: What would you say distinguishes the path of Sufism as brought by Hazrat Inayat Khan from other paths then?

Pir Netanel: What distinguishes the path of Sufism brought by Hazrat Inayat Khan? Being the "religion of the heart,"[2] as he puts it, I believe it is in touch with both the individual heart of the human being and the sacred heart at the center of all being, thus allowing for the uniqueness of individual experience and an experience of the divine pulse reverberating through and encompassing everything.

Moreover, the "message," as brought by Hazrat Inayat Khan, provides a spiritual umbrella under which all might come and find shelter.[3]

Question: Do you think there is anything unique or significantly different about Sufism and the spiritual path today, than say, three or four hundred years ago in Afghanistan or Turkey? Different challenges? Possibilities? Approaches to training? What feels enduring about the tradition or the path, and what elements may be evolving in relation to the times and culture?

Pir Netanel: I would be a fool to say it is 'the same,' but it would not be entirely right to say it 'it is different,' either. The philosopher Gerald Heard (quoting Ernst Haeckel) would say, "ontogeny recapitulates phylogeny." For him, this meant that the psycho-spiritual development of the individual (ontogeny) reflects the evolution of culture (phylogeny), and vice versa. That is to say, there is a developmental capacity or potential within us that is mirrored in the development of human society and culture as a whole. Or, just as we grow up as individuals, so, too, does humanity over a longer timeline.[4]

Without going into the whole presentation of this idea, I will just say that, in terms of developmental capacity, Sufis today are largely the same as those of the past. We have the same *basic* physical and psychological needs, as well as spiritual potentials. At the same time, more of that potential seems to have been actuated for us as a species through the millennia, and accompanied by the means of accumulating knowledge. As we have accumulated knowledge, or history, you might say, our external lives have changed drastically, at least in many parts of the world. And those changes mean that we have to approach many things somewhat differently than we did in the past, including Sufism.

Today, we live in a time-contracted world, flooded with an overwhelming amount of information, demanding a somewhat different approach to spiritual practice, and a refining and adaptation of our 'tools' to meet the needs of this time. It is also necessary to "increase the yield" of those tools—as my *murshid* put it—so that we can use them more effectively in a shorter amount of time. We must also adapt the presentation of the Sufi message to make it more accessible to where people are now.

Is Sufism itself different? Not in essence; but certainly in form. Form evolves over time. There are clear differences in the form of Sufism in various periods, from its early ascetic phase to the love-oriented flowering of the Sufi orders in the medieval period to our own day. Nevertheless, the orientation to the heart and remembrance remain the same.

I would also say that *'relationship'* is crucial to this paradigm, exploring spirituality in the context of our relationships. Almost none of the traditions have really dealt with relationships in any significant way, always seeing spiritual development in individual masculine or group terms. But development *vis-a-vis* another person is an integral part of this paradigm.

Suffering on the Spiritual Path

Question: Talk to us about personal sadness. As you ripen spiritually, does sadness go away? Does the nature of your sadness change? Is it realistic to expect that the spiritual path would result in happiness?

Pir Netanel: Well, if sadness is supposed to go away as a result of 'spiritual ripening,' then I suppose I haven't ripened to any appreciable degree. Sadness is simply a part of the human experience. A spirituality without it is, in some sense, *in-human* as far as I am concerned.

Does the experience of sadness change? I don't know; I think it feels the same. But maybe the conclusions we draw from it change. There is no need to reject it or call it 'bad.' It may feel unbearable, but it is not something that one should be ashamed of or reject. Sadness is a testimony to our humanity and how keenly we feel. It is an aspect of our relationship to love. It has to be known in the context of love.

In the Hasidic tradition, the 'broken heart' is understood as something valuable, precious. Only a heart that knows pain can be sensitive to another's pain. The story is told of the holy Apter Rav, Reb Avraham Yehoshua Heschel of Apt, who was once asked why his prayers always worked when those of others did not. He said: "When someone comes to me with their pain, with their problems, it makes a small hole in my heart. And now, after so many years, when I pray, I simply lift up my heart before God, this sad heart full of holes, and God cannot but feel pity and respond."[5]

Now this, by all accounts, was a great spiritual master. Was he happy? How can we know that? I do not see why the spiritual path should necessarily result in happiness. We certainly desire it; but is it a necessary outcome of the spiritual path? That may depend on what we mean by the word, 'happiness.' If it is an endless sunny day, untouched by grief or sadness, then likely not. But if it is something that can hold the complex co-existence of both sadness and gratitude, then I think perhaps that is something the spiritual path can help us to achieve.

Again, I would tend to think in terms of wholeness rather than happiness.

Question: Does suffering in the world, and in your personal life, affect your faith in the 'loving God,' the 'God of perfection'? If not, how does that work for you? Is there a place inside that we can reach beyond denial, despair, or spiritual platitude?

Pir Netanel: In *my* life? Without a doubt. Suffering has certainly affected my faith, and even caused a crisis of faith. I'm not embarrassed to say that I have hated God in the past, felt poison in my veins about the so-called 'God of love' who would send "his only begotten son"—as it says in the Gospels (John 3:16)—to be crucified on the cross. Suffering has burned away all the spiritual platitudes I used to repeat about 'a larger vision of God's justice.'

When you think about it, what do we really know about 'God's justice' and 'the greater meaning' of events? Such things may exist, and probably do from my perspective; but what do we really *know* about them? The scale of God's justice is just too big for our limited vision. From where we stand in our suffering, as we stand in the middle of it, *God is not just . . . God is cruel.* That is our experience sometimes, and it is valid. It is only in 'spiritual hindsight' that we gain perspective and make meaning out of these events. We shouldn't try to bypass the difficult reality of our painful unknowing and limited vision in the moment, for we grow in the struggle of those experiences.

There was once a Hasidic master who sat unseen, late at night, in a dark corner of an inn before the Day of Atonement. He watched as the innkeeper sat down at a table and took out a ledger. The innkeeper opened the ledger and said, "God, these are all my offences for the year . . ." and he went on to list them one-by-one. Then, unexpectedly, he took out a second ledger and said, "But these are all your offences against us . . ." and he listed all the bad things that had happened to him and the community that same year. In the end, he closed both ledgers and said, "Perhaps, God, we should call it even?"[6]

You see, in the Hasidic tradition, you can also make demands of God, and must, because the truth is, God owes us as much as we owe God.

We need to be careful about washing over our pain with convenient spiritual explanations and talk that makes us feel good, but that is not necessarily substantiated in a way that builds a solid spiritual foundation. You see, it is not that I really had an idea of a personal God anymore when I began to suffer; that was long since gone. But there were vestiges of unexamined beliefs and ideas that exploded under the intense heat of suffering in my life, leaving something more painful, though also more real and profound. I knew then the terribly sublime vision that Krishna showed to Arjuna of the totality of being, in all its beauty and ugliness, and I both loved and hated it.[7] And somehow, afterward, though I loved the *'God'* of my youth less, I loved God in the world more. I was returned to a richer experience of love.

Spiritual Practice

Question: Let's say that one person meditates consistently for thirty years, while another prays diligently for thirty years. What kind of person does each become? How are they different? Are both orientations included in this path, and given the same emphasis?

Pir Netanel: I don't think we know that they will be different at all. It depends on the individual, their natural tendencies, and where they started. But if we are trying to take the *'all things being equal'* stance, then we might speculate in the following way. Prayer, being an expressive activity, is generally considered "positive" in Hazrat Inayat Khan's terms, while meditation, being generally inward, might be considered a "negative" method.[8] (I'm not talking about positive and negative in terms of value judgments, such as good and bad, but in descriptive terms, such as when we talk about positive and negative space.) Prayer, as extemporaneous activity, or even recitation, is expressive, and can be seen as 'clearing the pipes,' for we are expressive beings.

A *murid* once asked me, "What does God need our prayer for?" That is to say, if God is worthy of the name, then there is no need for us to say anything in the first place, right? But the answer to the question is simple: God may not need our prayer, but we need to pray, because we are expressive beings; we express outward.

Meditation, on the other hand, is a means of attuning consciousness. It also allows us to discern an authentic voice amid the cacophony of voices within us, a voice that is truly ours, that represents our deepest self or Self.

I would say that we need both—the positive and expressive activity of prayer, and the negative, interior activity of meditation—to live a fully realized spiritual life, like two poles between which we must run back and forth. But that is just my opinion.

Extemporaneous prayer has not been as emphasized in Inayati Sufism, though I would recommend it as good for the soul, and I cannot think of a single reason why it should not be emphasized here. After all, it was practiced by the great Sufi saint, Rabi'a al-Adawiyya, and many other Sufis through the centuries. In the Hasidic tradition, we see a profound example of its use in the teachings of Rebbe Nahman of Bratzlav, who calls it *hitbodedut.* It is also strongly emphasized in Protestant Christianity.

Question: Sometimes ideas are taught that I don't necessarily connect with or understand. I want to be real about my spirituality. I don't want to pretend that I feel a connection to these things when I don't. For example, tuning-in to angelic beings. I'm not sure I know what that means. If I don't experience these things, how do I relate to them? Is there a way to make them more real?

Pir Netanel: We either have to make them more real, or move on from talking about them altogether. If we take the example of angelic beings, we have to get to the heart of the esoteric teachings around them, and find a way to apply those teachings in our actual lives. For instance, the word, *malak*, in Arabic, means 'messenger.' The angel is a messenger, the carrier of a message. But the esoteric teachings also tell us that the angel is itself the message, birthed in a given moment by our actions, emotions, or thoughts, carrying our deep intentions to other planes of reality, where a response is crafted, which is itself an angelic *'messenger-message.'* If we understand the implications of this teaching, then we might look differently at our less noble actions, emotions, and thoughts, considering the angelic-messages with which we are seeding the womb of the universe, and considering what kind of child will come from them.

Otherwise, talk of angels usually seems to me, as my *murshid* put it—elaborating on Fritz Perls' categories of "chicken shit" (inconsequential talk), "bull shit" (lies and exaggeration), and "elephant shit" (grandiose talk and intellectual bypassing)—just so much "angel shit," airy-fairy spiritual talk without much substance or meaning.[9]

Question: What does it mean to be a 'friend of God'? How does one become God's friend?

Pir Netanel: That is about *qurb* (proximity) or *uns* (intimacy) in Sufism. It is to be so close to God, to have such an intimate relationship, that God is like one's closest, most reliable and intimate friend or companion.

Friendship is one of the root metaphors of Sufism. We use specific language to define a particular quality of relationship cultivated on the Sufi path. For instance, one could address God as 'father,' 'mother,' 'king,' or even 'boss,' and get into the mode of those specific relationships and their qualities. But Sufism tends to cultivate a relationship with God as 'friend' or 'beloved,' emphasizing intimacy and love.

Question: If someone were coming to you sincerely about embarking on the spiritual path, what tips from your own hard won experience would you give them about how to make their way?

Pir Netanel: Watch your integrity. Pay attention to that. Take responsibility for your own path, and do not place responsibility for it on anyone else, no matter how "realized" you think they might be.

Notes

Chapter 1: The Story of Sufism

1. A parable attributed to Khwaja Yusuf Hamadani by Idries Shah. A less elaborate version of the story is given in Shah's *Tales of the Dervishes.* London: Jonathan Cape, 1967: 88-90. After originally reading this story in Shah, I went on to tell it for many years, often as way of introducing Sufism. After some years, I needed to consult the original to confirm a detail, only to discover that I had greatly embroidered it. However, I was pleased to note that I had preserved all of the essentials, as well as the most important details and phrases. Left out is the section of the parable on poisons and false teas.

2. A traditional Sufi saying.

3. Muzaffer Ozak. *Love is the Wine: Talks of a Sufi Master in America.* Ed. Ragip Frager. Putney, VT: Threshold Books, 1987: 1.

4. This is a common practice in many Sufi texts.

5. See A.J. Arberry. *The Doctrine of the Sufis.* Lahore: Sh. Muhammad Ashraf, 1966: 5, and Al-Hujwiri. *Revelation of the Mystery (Kashf al-Mahjub).* Tr. Reynold A. Nicholson. Accord, NY: Pir Press, 1999: 30.

6. Martin Lings. *Muhammad: His Life Based on the Earliest Sources.* Rochester, VT: Inner Traditions International, 1983: 167.

7. Jeffrey Mishlove. "Irina Tweedie: The Sufi Path." *Thinking Allowed.* 1998. (Video)

8. Attributed to Abu'l-Hasan Fushanja (8th/9th-century) by Abu'l-Hasan al-Hujwiri in *Kashf al-Mahjub.* See Al-Hujwiri, *Revelation of the Mystery,* 44. Also attributed to Junayd of Baghdad. See Fadhlalla Haeri. *The Elements of Sufism.* Barnes and Noble Books, 1999: 14.

9. See Arberry, *The Doctrine of the Sufis,* 5, and Al-Hujwiri, *Revelation of the Mystery,* 30.

10. See Ibid., 5, and Al-Hujwiri, *Revelation of the Mystery,* 30.

11. Louis Massignon. "Tasawwuf." *Encyclopedia of Islam: 1st Edition.* Eds. M. Th. Houtsma, T.W. Arnold, R. Basset and R. Hartmann. Leiden: E.J. Brill, 1913-1938: 313.

12. A.J. Arberry. *Sufism: An Account of the Mystics of Islam.* London, England: George Allen & Unwin Ltd., 1950: 37.

13. Greek, *essaioi,* a corruption of the Aramaic, *hasya,* or Hebrew, *hasidim.*

14. Arberry, *Sufism,* 37. Massignon, "Tasawwuf," 313-14.

15. "Do not frequent the company of kings and princes." Hasan Lufti Shushud. *Masters of Wisdom of Central Asia: Teachings from the Path of Liberation.* Tr. Muhtar Holland. Rochester, VT: Inner Traditions, 2014: 30.

16. By the 9th-century, the name "Sufi" came to apply to all the *nussak.* In Khurasan and Transoxania (Central Asia), they were also called *hakim* (pl. *hukama')* also *'arif* (pl. *'arifun), fakir,* and *darwish.* Massignon, "Tasawwuf," 313-14. Arberry, *Sufism,* 35.

17. Al-Rudhabari, 9th-century.

18. A traditional Sufi saying.

19. See Farid ad-Din 'Attar. *Farid ad-Din 'Attar's Memorial of God's Friends.* Tr. Paul Losensky. New York: Paulist Press, 2009: 99.

20. See Widad El Sakkakini. *First Among Sufis: The Life and Thought of Rabia al-Adawiyya, the Woman Saint of Basra.* London: The Octagon Press, 1982: 62.

21. See 'Attar, *Farid ad-Din 'Attar's Memorial of God's Friends,* 113.

22. See Annemarie Schimmel. *Mystical Dimensions of Islam.* Chapel Hill, NC: University of North Carolina Press, 1975: 38-39.

23. Such ecstatic outbursts are called, *shathiyat* (sing. *shath).*

24. This is the classic story of Mansur al-Hallaj's martyrdom. The historical truth is more complex. It seems that he inspired a movement of moral and political reform in Baghdad which made him powerful enemies. He was then forced to flee Baghdad. He was later arrested and imprisoned for nine years and finally condemned as being part of an insurgent group who wished to destroy the *ka'bah.* He had said, "Circle the *ka'bah* of the heart seven times," and some also reported that he said cities should build local ka'bahs for people to circumambulate. For these things, he was denounced. But ash-Shafi'i,

the greatest Muslim jurist of the time, refused to condemn him, saying that mystic inspiration was beyond his jurisdiction. Nevertheless, he was condemned by the government. The queen-mother interceded and the order was revoked, but the vizier continued conniving until al-Hallaj was finally condemned, tortured, hanged, and decapitated in Baghdad. His last words were said to be, "The only thing that matters is to be absorbed in Unity."

25. The parable of tea is attributed to the Khwajaghan, who are said to have been critical of al-Hallaj, considering his public *shath* an example of spiritual imprudence. They were advocates of quiet work out of the public eye. "'If at his time even one of [Khwaja 'Abd al-Khaliq Ghujdawani's] disciples had been on the spot, [Mansur al-Hallaj'] would not have got into trouble. He would have put [al-Hallaj] in his place and got rid of his nonsense.'" J.G. Bennett. *Gurdjieff: Making a New World.* New York, NY: Harper & Row Publishers, 1973: 37-38.

26. Actually, this is my own paraphrase of Murshid Samuel Lewis' paraphrase of Al-Ghazzali, "Sufism consists of experiences not premises." *Sufi Vision and Initiation Meetings with Remarkable Beings.* Ed. Neil Douglas-Klotz. San Francisco: Sufi Islamia/Prophecy Publications, 1986: 19. It seems to be based on a whole passage in *Al-Munqidh min ad-Dalal* of Abu Hamid al-Ghazzali. One sentence (in Watt's translation) reads: "It became clear to me, however, that what is most distinctive of mysticism is something which cannot be apprehended by study, but only by immediate experience *(dhawq*—literally, 'tasting'), by ecstasy and by a moral change." W. Montgomery Watt. *The Faith and Practice of Al-Ghazali.* London: George Allen & Unwin Ltd., 1953: 54-55.

27. Inayat Khan. *The Unity of Religious Ideals.* Part II, "The God-Ideal."

28. Inayat Khan. *The Sufi Message of Hazrat Inayat Khan: Volume 12: The Vision of God and Man.* Geneva: International Headquarters of the Sufi Movement, 1982: 150.

29. Inayat Khan. "America, 1910-1912." *Autobiography.*

30. Inayat Khan. *Religious Gathekas.* #1.

31. This reminds me of the Bektashi saying reported by Murat Yagan. *I Come from Behind Calf Mountain.* Putney, VT: Threshhold Books, 1984: 155: Sufism is the "process of awakening and developing latent human powers under Divine Grace and guidance."

32. Reproduced in many places. See Hakim Moinuddin Chishti. *The Book of Sufi Healing.* Rochester, VT: Inner Traditions, 1991: 9.

Chapter 2: Circling the Temple of God

1. This is an adaptation of the "external zikrs" of Hazrat Inayat Khan. *Sangithas.* (Privately Circulated) The placement of the hands, creating a symbolic eagle and winged heart, as well as this last phrase, "This is the temple of the heart," are particular adaptations of the Inayati-Maimuni lineage.

2. Or *dhikr* (the dh is a soft th sound).

3. "Zikr is the process of repeating the sacred word with concentration, that it may impress on the entire self of the one who repeats it the meaning of the word." Inayat Khan. *Githas.* Riyazat: No. 6. (Privately Circulated).

4. Tor Andrae. *Mohammed: The Man and His Faith.* Tr. Theophil Menzel. New York: Harper & Brothers, 1960: 13-30.

5. Martin Buber. *Israel and the World: Essays in a Time of Crisis.* New York: Schocken Books, 1948: 21-24.

6. "The seeker must recite *[zikr]* by negation and affirmation on his tongue until he reaches the state of the contemplation of his heart. That state will be achieved by reciting every day the negation *([La 'ilaha])* and affirmation *(['illa llah])* on the tongue, between 5,000 and 10,000 times, removing from his heart the elements that rust and tarnish it." Muhammad Hisham Kabbani. *Classical Islam and the Naqshbandi Sufi Tradition.* Fenton, MI: Islamic Supreme Council of America, 2004: 170.

7. "Number four: The ['h'] at the end of *[Allah]* attended with a ['u']—God's reply to one's invocation—comes in the form of the pronoun in the third person: him, person not present." Vilayat Inayat Khan. *Toward the One.* New York: Harper & Row Publishers, 1974: 310. "That's what the *[zikr]* is about, to make God present, and that's the meaning of *[hu].*" Vilayat Inayat Khan. "The Practice of Dhikr." *Chishtia Inayati Dhikr.* Sufi Order International (privately printed booklet), ca. 2000: 6.

8. "The mode of recitation of the *[zikr]* varies from school to school. Here is the method followed by the Sufis. There are actually four stages." Inayat Khan, *Toward the One,* 304.

9. "While reciting, the head is moved in the motion of an arc, starting with the left cheek resting upon the left shoulder. The head is then swung downward across the chest, and a pause is made with the face looking upward. This is done as *[La 'ilaha]* is uttered." Hakim Moinuddin Chishti. *The Book of Sufi Healing*. Rochester, VT: Inner Traditions, 1991:144. "[...] turn the head in a half-circle from the left shoulder, circling downward to the left knee, then moving to the right knee, then upward to the right shoulder. Continue to rotate the head to the zenith. As you are making this circular motion, think of the words, *[La 'ilaha],* or, in English, 'There is no other Divinity.'" Vilayat Inayat Khan. *Awakening: A Sufi Experience.* New York: Jeremy P. Tarcher, 1999: 175. "Start making a circle as you exhale and say *[La]* as you slowly move your head in a circular fashion. Your head faces your left shoulder, and if you are sitting cross-legged, it faces your left knee then your right knee, your right shoulder and finally right up towards [the] zenith." Inayat Khan, "The Practice of Dhikr," 1-2. "Number One: *[La 'ilaha],* there is no divinity. The *[La]* is intoned while describing a circular motion of the head: third eye facing left shoulder, solar plexus, right shoulder. *['Ilaha]* is intoned as one reaches upwards to the apex of the circle." Inayat Khan, *Toward the One,* 304.

10. I am reminded of the song, "Silence," with its simple, heartfelt lyrics, struggling with the necessity of a hidden God: "Got to crush my fantasies / of how this life is supposed to be; / bring my broken heart to an invisible king / with a hope, one day, you might answer me; / so I pray, 'Don't you abandon me!' / Your silence kills me . . . / I wouldn't have it any other way. / Is it wrong to think you might speak to me? / You might speak, would it be words, / and what would you say? / It's so heavy, a heavy price to pay— / Your silence." Matisyahu. "Silence." *Light.* Epic/JDub, 2010.

11. "Then, as the syllable *['illa]* is voiced, the head is thrown rather forcefully downward in the direction of the heart." Chishti, *The Book of Sufi Healing,* 144. "Then, [...] turn your head downward toward the solar plexus..." Inayat Khan, *Awakening,* 175. "Now if you just let your head follow that impulse, you can feel the pull of the void as your head reaches down toward the solar plexus." Inayat Khan,

"The Practice of Dhikr," 3. "Number Two: *['Illa],* except [...] This is intoned while thrusting the head downwards like an arrow, the third eye facing the solar plexus." Inayat Khan, *Toward the One,* 306.

12. Johnny Lee. "Lookin' for Love." *Urban Cowboy.* Full Moon Records, 1980.

13. A treasured Sufi *ḥadith,* possibly based on the Qur'an, Surah 59:19: "Do not be like those who forgot *Allah,* who made them forget themselves."

14. "[...] immediately raise your head straight up again in line with the spine [...] with the face turned upward. With this [...] motion, think of the second half of the phrase, *['illa llah]*—'except God.'" Inayat Khan, *Awakening,* 175.

15. Inayat Khan. *The Unity of Religious Ideals.* Part II, "The God-Ideal."

16. "Number Three: *[Allah] ([Llah])* [...] This is the great proc lamation, the pronouncement of the great name of God: the supreme moment of glorification, one's participation in the cosmic Hallelujah which originated all forms." Inayat Khan, *Toward the One,* 307.

17. "Now [...] turn your head toward your physical heart, thinking the word, *[hu].*" Inayat Khan, *Awakening,* 175. "Now, if you say *[hu],* the head turns back toward the heart center." Inayat Khan, "The Practice of Dhikr," 6. "Later on you place the *[hu]* in the heart chakra [...]." Vilayat Inayat Khan. "Aspects of the Dhikr." *Chishtia Inayati Dhikr.* Sufi Order International (privately printed booklet), ca. 2000: 15.

18. Zia Inayat-Khan. *Saracen Chivalry: Counsels on Valor, Generosity and the Mystical Quest.* New Lebanon, NY: Suluk Press, 2012: 12.

19. "Consider *[zikr]* as a prayer." Inayat Khan, "The Practice of Dhikr," *Chishtia Inayati Dhikr,* 1.

20. "The second aspect of the *zikr* is to make a form on one's body a certain psychical design [...]" Khan, *Sangithas.* (Privately Circulated)

21. *Sahih Muslim.* 131.

22. "The first aspect is the clear and correct repetition of the *zikr: [La 'ilaha 'illa llah hu]* [...]" Khan, *Sangithas.* (Privately Circulated)

23. "In *zikr,* the thought is kept on all the syllables and sounds, making it difficult to think of anything else." Khan, *Githas,* Dhyana: No. 4. (Privately Circulated)

24. "Remember with the heart at the same time as mentioning with the tongue—or transforming *[zikr]* of the tongue into *[zikr]* of the heart." Hasan Lufti Shushud. *Masters of Wisdom of Central Asia: Teachings from the Sufi Path of Liberation*. Tr. Muhtar Holland. Rochester, VT: 2014: 32.

25. "The third aspect of the *zikr* is to think of the meaning." Khan, *Sangithas.* (Privately Circulated)

26. "If the *zikr* becomes automatic and is recited without proper thought and feeling, it still is of value because of the intrinsic power of the atoms responding to sound. Besides that, it harmonizes one with the atmosphere and attunes one with all *zikr* atmosphere, so one cannot continue the practice without developing out of it the necessary thought and feeling which will then carry one along." Khan, *Githas,* Dhyana: No. 4. (Privately Circulated)

27. "*Zikr* has one great advantage over all other practices. That is, in the body and mind both, the re-echo of *zikr* is produced, and both planes of the zakir's being are set to rhythm. Music constitutes rhythm and tone; and if they are both produced by the means of *zikr* in one's body and mind, the very being of the *zakir* becomes musical." Ibid., Riyazat: No. 8.

28. This beautiful description of *zikr* by Ghazzali is given in Massud Farzan. *The Tale of the Reed Pipe: Teachings of the Sufis.* New York: E.P. Dutton & Co., 1974: 51-52. However, he cites it as coming from *Deliverance from Error.* I can find no trace of it there.

29. "If you follow what is said above, you can be sure that the light of Truth will dawn upon your heart. At first intermittently, like flashes of lightning, it will come and go. Sometimes when it comes back it may stay longer than other times. Sometimes it may stay only briefly." Ghazzali in Massud Farzan, *The Tale of the Reed Pipe,* 52.

30. See Farid ad-Din 'Attar. *Farid ad-Din 'Attar's Memorial of God's Friends.* Tr. Paul Losensky. New York: Paulist Press, 2009: 346.

31. Inayat Khan, *Awakening,* 176.

32. Inayat Khan, "The Practice of Dhikr," 2.

33. Ibid., 2, 3.

34. This is an adaptation of the "external zikrs" of Khan, *Sangithas.* (Privately Circulated) The placement of the hands, creating a

symbolic eagle and winged heart are particular adaptations of the Inayati-Maimuni lineage.

Chapter 3: The Chain of Transmission

1. Carl W. Ernst, and Bruce B. Lawrence. *Sufi Martyrs of Love: The Chishti Order in South Asia and Beyond.* New York, NY: Palgrave Macmillan, 2002: 19-20.

2. Zia Inayat-Khan. *Tree of Lights: The Chishti Lineage of Hazrat Inayat Khan.* Richmond, VA: The Inayati Order, 2018: 21-22.

3. Ernst, *Sufi Martyrs of Love,* 19.

4. As reported in the traditional hagiographies. See Ibid., 149.

5. See Inayat Khan. *The Sufi Message: Volume X: Sufi Mysticism*. Delhi: Motilal Banarsidass Publishers, 1990: 64-66.

6. See Inayat-Khan, *Tree of Lights,* 43-44.

7. Ibid., 64. K.A. Nizami. "Chishtiyya." *Encyclopedia of Islam.* (Vol. 2). Leiden: E.J. Brill, 1960: 55.

8. Scott Kugle (ed.). *Sufi Meditation and Contemplation: Timeless Wisdom from Mughal India.* Tr. Scott Kugle and Carl Ernst. New Lebanon, NY: Suluk Press, 2012: 18.

9. Published in English translation in Kugle, *Sufi Meditation and Contemplation,* 18.

10. Ernst, *Sufi Martyrs of Love,* 142. Kugle, *Sufi Meditation and Contemplation.* 18.

11. Ibid., 142-43.

12. Ibid., 142-43, 128-29.

13. Ibid., 28. Kugle, *Sufi Meditation and Contemplation,* 31-32, and Pir Rasheed-ul-Hasan Kaleemi's preface, xii.

14. Inayat Khan's "Confessions" in Inayat Khan. *The Sufi Message: Volume XII: The Divinity of the Human Soul.* Delhi: Motilal Banarsidass Publishers, 1990: 149. Even the revered modern Chishti master, Pir Rasheed-ul-Hasan Jeeli-ul-Kaleemi (d. 2013), has written that the Kalimi branch of the Chishti lineage combined the four schools of

Sufism "into one path, trying to take the best of each." Kugle, *Sufi Meditation and Contemplation,* xiv.

15. Muhyiddin Ibn 'Arabi. *Sufis of Andalusia: The Ruh al-Quds & al-Durrat at-Fakhirah.* Tr. R.W. J. Austin. Roxburgh, Great Britain: Beshara Publications, 2002.

16. Ernst, *Sufi Martyrs of Love,* 50.

17. Annmarie Schimmel. *Mystical Dimensions of Islam.* Chapel Hill, NC: University of North Carolina Press, 1975: 38.

18. Annmarie Schimmel. *My Soul is a Woman: The Feminine in Islam.* New York, NY: Continuum, 1997: 50.

19. Shaykh Javad Nurbakhsh has given us a work on *Sufi Women,* Shaykha Camille Helminski has written *Women of Sufism: A Hidden Treasure,* and Tamam Kahn has written *Untold: A History of the Wives of Prophet Muhammad.*

20. Although the title, *Tree of Lights: The Chishti Lineage of Hazrat Inayat Khan,* bears resemblance to the title of the 19th-century book of Chishti hagiography, *Shajarat al-Anvar,* which has the same meaning, that book has never been translated and exists only in manuscript. The material in Pir Zia's small book is original and not a translation of the former work. It was been transcribed from oral talks by Pir Zia (ca. 2000), and was originally edited for a private publication and made available to murids in 2001. Recently, it was re-edited by myself and Pir Zia so that Inayati murids may once more have the benefit of accessing this information and studying their own lineage.

21. Inayat-Khan, *Tree of Lights,* 22.

22. See Basira Beardsworth. *Chishti Sufis of Dehli in the Lineage of Hazrat Pir-o-Murshid Inayat Khan.* Private publication, 2013: 11.

23. Inayat-Khan, *Tree of Lights,* 51.

24. Zia Inayat Khan. "The 'Silsila-i Sufian': From Khwaja Mu'in al-Din Chishti to Sayyid Abu Hashim Madani." *A Pearl in Wine: Essays on the Life, Music and Sufism of Hazrat Inayat Khan.* Ed. Zia Inayt Khan. New Lebanon, NY: Omega Publications, 2001: 292.

25. Inayat-Khan, *Tree of Lights,* 5.

26. K.A. Nizami. "Introduction." *Morals for the Heart: Conversations of Shaykh Nizam ad-din Awliya Recorded by Amir Hasan Sijizi.* Nizam ad-Din Awliya. Tr. Bruce B. Lawrence. New York, NY: Paulist Press, 1992: 19-20.

27. Paraphrase of Nizam ad-Din Awliya, *Morals for the Heart,* 103.

28. Ibid., 354.

29. Carl E. Ernst (ed.). *Teachings of Sufism.* Boston, MA; Shambhala Publications, 1999: 194-99.

30. Ernst, *Teachings of Sufism,* 194-95.

31. This was accomplished in 2018.

32. Inayat Khan. *Biography of Pir-o-Murshid Inayat Khan.* London: East-West Publications, 1979: 243.

Chapter 4: Eight Principles of Sufi Mindfulness

1. Adapted from the original version found in Inayat Khan. *The Divinity of the Human Soul: The Sufi Message Series.* "Confessions," Chapter 4.

2. See Khan, "Confessions," Chapter 4.

3. Attributed to Abu'l-Hasan Fushanja (8th/9th-century) by Abu'l-Hasan al-Hujwiri in *Kashf al-Mahjub.* See Al-Hujwiri, *Revelation of the Mystery (Kashf al-Mahjub).* Tr. Reynold A. Nicholson. Accord, NY: Pir Press, 1999: 44. Also attributed to Junayd of Baghdad. See Fadhlalla Haeri. *The Elements of Sufism.* Barnes and Noble Books, 1999: 14.

4. According to J.G. Bennett, *khwaja* "originally meant 'possessed of superior learning.' The word was of Persian origin and never used in Arab counties. The chief Wazir of the Samanid kings was called the *Khwaja-i Buzurg* and his insignia of office was an inkstand." J.G. Bennett. *The Masters of Wisdom.* London: Turnstone Books, 1977: Note on 121.

5. See Bennett. *The Masters of Wisdom,* 116-38.

6. "Nor were they at all favourable to ecstasies and mystical raptures. One of the sayings of Khwaja Azizan Ali illustrates this: 'If at his time even one of [Khwaja 'Abd al-Khaliq Ghujdawani's] disciples had been on the spot, [Mansur al-Hallaj] would not have got into trouble. He would have put [al-Hallaj] in his place and got rid of his nonsense.'" J.G. Bennett. *Gurdjieff: Making a New World.* New York, NY: Harper & Row Publishers, 1973: 37-38. The original from which Bennett is translating is more subtle in its criticism: "If a son of [Khwaja 'Abd al-Khaliq] had been alive at that time, [Mansur al-Hallaj would not have gone to the gallows, for he would have trained the cotton-carder

and save him from our fate." Hasan Lufti Shushud. *Masters of Wisdom of Central Asia: Teachings from the Path of Liberation.* Tr. Muhtar Holland. Rochester, VT: Inner Traditions, 2014: 41. Khwaja 'Abd al-Khaliq Ghujdawani is also reported to have said, "Do not seek fame, for in fame lies calamity" and "Do not frequent the company of kings and princes." Shushud. *Masters of Wisdom of Central Asia,* 30. These latter sentiments are fully consistent with the views of the early Chishti Sufis, perhaps demonstrating some level of relationship.

7. Bennett. *The Masters of Wisdom,* 119, 122, 129.

8. Ibid., 131.

9. In the words of Najm ad-Din Kubra: "The 'h' in the divine name *[Allah]* is the very sound we make with every breath. The other letters (in the Arabic spelling: *alif* and reduplicated *lam)* represent an intensified definite article (serving to emphasize the Uniqueness of God). The essential part of the divine name is therefore 'h,' which automatically accompanies our breath. All life depends on the constant utterance of that noble name." Shushud, *Masters of Wisdom of Central Asia,* 31.

10. This quote is given in a variety of ways. Inayat Khan. *Sufi Teachings: The Art of Being: The Sufi Message Series.* "Health and Order of Body and Mind," Chapter 17: "My spiritual teacher, my Murshid, once said, 'People say that there are many sins and virtues, but I think there is only one sin.' I asked him what it was, and he said, 'To let one breath go without being conscious of it.'" Inayat Khan. *The Unity of Religious Ideals: The Sufi Message Series.* Part II ("God the Infinite"): "My *murshid,* Abu Hashim Madani, once said that there is only one virtue and only one sin for a soul on this path: virtue when he is conscious of God and sin when he is not."

11. Muhammad Hisham Kabbani. *Classical Islam and the Naqshbandi Sufi Tradition.* Fenton, MI: Islamic Supreme Council of America, 2004: 165. In Bennett, *Gurdjieff,* 34, he says: "Do not let your attention wander for the duration of a single breath. Remember yourself always and in all situations."

12. "Sound, Spirit and Gender in the Qur'an" in Michael S. Sells (tr.), *Approaching the Qur'an: The Early Revelations.* Ashland, OR: White Cloud Press, 1999: 183-207.

13. "*[Zikr]* is flowing in the body of every single living creature by the necessity of their breath—even without will—as a sign of obedience,

which is part of their creation. Through their breathing, the sound of *'[huwa]'* of the Divine Name of God is made with every exhalation and inhalation and it is a sign of the Unseen Essence serving to emphasize the Uniqueness of God. Therefore, it is necessary to be present with that breathing, in order to realize the essence of the Creator. [...] "The name *['Allah']* which encompasses the Ninety-Nine Names and Attributes consists of four letters: *alif, lam, lam* and *ha (Allah).* The people of Sufism say that the Absolute Unseen Essence of God, Exalted and Mighty, is expressed by the last letter as vowelized by the *alif, ['huwa.']* The first *lam* is for the sake of emphasis. Safeguarding your breath from heedlessness will lead you to complete Presence." Kabbani, *Classical Islam and the Naqshbandi Sufi Tradition,* 166.

14. "This Order is built on breath. So it is a must for everyone to safeguard his breath in the time of his inhalation and exhalation, and further, to safeguard his breath in the interval between the inhalation and exhalation." Ibid., 166. "In this path, the foundation is built upon breathing. The more one is able to be conscious of one's breathing, the stronger is one's inner life." Bennett. *The Masters of Wisdom,* 134. "The external basis of this *[tariqah]* is the breath." J. Spencer Trimingham. *The Sufi Orders in Islam.* New York, NY: Oxford University Press, 1971: 203.

15. Idries Shah. *A Perfumed Scorpion.* London: The Octagon Press, 1978: 86.

16. Shushud, *Masters of Wisdom of Central Asia,* 32.

17. Kabbani, *Classical Islam and the Naqshbandi Sufi Tradition,* 167.

18. Ibid., 168.

19. Bennett, *The Masters of Wisdom,* 135.

20. "I have met with but one or two persons in the course of my life who understood the art of Walking, that is, of taking walks, who had a genius, so to speak, for *sauntering;* which word is beautifully derived 'from idle people who roved about the country, in the Middle Ages, and asked charity, under pretense of going *à la Sainte Terre,'* to the Holy Land, till the children exclaimed, 'There goes a *Sainte-Terrer,'* a Saunterer, a Holy-Lander. They who never go to the Holy Land in their walks, as they pretend, are indeed mere idlers and vagabonds; but they who do go there are saunterers in the good sense, such as I mean. [...] I walk out into Nature such as the old prophets and poets,

Menu, Moses, Homer, Chaucer, walked in. [...] I believe that there is a subtle magnetism in Nature, which, if we unconsciously yield to it, will direct us aright." Henry David Thoreau, "Walking." *Walden and Other Writings of Henry David Thoreau.* Ed. Brooks Atkinson. New York: The Modern Library, 1965: 597, 604, 607.

21. Trimingham. *The Sufi Orders in Islam,* 203.

22. A simple description of Sufi walking meditation coordinated with the breath (but without the *wazifa)* is given by my meditation teacher, Puran Bair, in his *Living from the Heart: Heart Rhythm Meditation for Energy, Clarity, Peace, Joy, and Inner Peace.* New York: Three Rivers Press, 1998: 147-48.

23. "Your journey is towards your homeland. Remember that you are traveling from the world of appearances to the World of Reality." Bennett, *Gurdjieff,* 34.

24. "The journey home. This is interpreted to mean the transformation that brings man out of the world of unrealized potential, *alam-i arvah,* to the world of will, *alam-i wujuub,* where man becomes aware of his destiny and is given the power to fulfill it. The *alam-i wujub* corresponds to the Kingdom of Heaven in the Gospels. The [Khwajaghan] taught that man can neither know nor realize his own destiny so long as he remains in the subjective dream state—*khayalat."* Bennett. *The Masters of Wisdom,* 135. "Pass from the world of potentiality to the world of realization." Shushud, *Masters of Wisdom of Central Asia,* 32.

25. "This is an interior journey, the movement from blameworthy to praiseworthy qualities. Others refer to it as the vision or revelation of the hidden side of the *shahada.*" Trimingham, *The Sufi Orders in Islam,* 203.

26. Kabbani, *Classical Islam and the Naqshbandi Sufi Tradition,* 168. *Safar dar vatan* is also described by Idries Shah as an "Exploration of the student's own mind by himself, establishing the watchfulness connected with the transformation of the Self." Shah, *A Perfumed Scorpion,* 86.

27. Shushud, *Masters of Wisdom of Central Asia,* 32. Moreover, "According to Khwaja Awliya' Kabir, it means that one should reach the stage where one is so constantly and completely absorbed in divine remembrance that 'one could walk through the market-place without hearing a sound.'" Ibid.

28. Ibid., 32.

29. "In all your outward activity remain inwardly free. Learn not to identify yourself with anything whatsoever." Bennett, *Gurdjieff*, 34.

30. "To be able to enter fully into the life of the external world without losing one's inner freedom. When asked for a short statement of the method of the Khwajaghan, [Khwaja Baha' ad-Din Naqshband] replied, *'[khilvat dar anjuman]*, that is, outwardly to be with the people and inwardly to be with God'. Khwaja Awliya' said that it means: 'to be so deeply occupied with one's own *zikr* that one can walk through the market place and not be aware of a sound.'" Bennett. *The Masters of Wisdom*, 135.

31. Kabbani, *Classical Islam and the Naqshbandi Sufi Tradition*, 169.

32. Rosenblatt, Samuel (ed. & tr.). *The High Ways to Perfection of Abraham Maimonides: Volume II.* Baltimore, MD: The Johns Hopkins Press, 1983: 383.

33. Trimingham. *The Sufi Orders in Islam*, 203.

34. Shushud, *Masters of Wisdom of Central Asia*, 32.

35. "It is the doing of *[zikr]*, which is the essence, or heart of remembrance" . . . "repeating *['Allah']*, the name of God's Essence that encompasses all other names and Attributes." Kabbani, *Classical Islam and the Naqshbandi Sufi Tradition*, 170.

36. "The explanation given in the *Rashahat* is that one must learn to keep contact between the tongue and the heart, especially in the *zikr*—what we feel we should say and what we say, we should feel." Bennett. *The Masters of Wisdom*, 135. "Remember with the heart at the same time as mentioning with the tongue—or transforming *[zikr]* of the tongue into *[zikr]* of the heart." Shushud, *Masters of Wisdom of Central Asia*, 32. "Remember your Friend, i.e., God. Let the prayer *(zikr)* of your tongue be the prayer of your heart *(q'alb)."* Bennett, *Gurdjieff*, 34.

37. This talk took place in the performing arts center of the Naropa Institute, Boulder, Colorado, ca. 1999. The translator may have been Jules Levinson.

38. Scott Kugel (ed.). *Sufi Meditation and Contemplation: Timeless Wisdom from Mughal India.* Tr. Scott Kugel and Carl Ernst. New Lebanon, NY: Suluk Press/ Omega Publications, 2012: 38.

39. "Other masters say it means 'return', 'repent', that is return to

al-Haqq by way of contrition *(inkisar)."* Trimingham. *The Sufi Orders in Islam,* 203.

40. "The *[zakir],* when engaging in the heart-repetition of the 'blessed phrase,' should intersperse it with such phrases as, 'My God, Thou art my Goal and Thy satisfaction is my aim', to help to keep one's thoughts from straying." The attribution to the Prophet Muḥammad apparently comes from Ghujdawani. Kabbani, *Classical Islam and the Naqshbandi Sufi Tradition,* 171. Shah Kalim Allah Jahanabadi says, "one must say in the heart, 'Oh God, you are my goal and I desire your contentment' *(Ilahi anta maqsudi wa rida'uka matlubi)."* Kugel, *Sufi Meditation and Contemplation:* 71.Trimingham. *The Sufi Orders in Islam,* 203. We may do this when we come to a counter bead on the *tesbiḥ,* or each time we become aware of drifting!

41. Paraphrasing the fourth Lubavitcher Rebbe, Rabbi Shmuel of Lubavitch (1834-1882), "One should try to act like a perfect *tzaddik (tzaddik gamur)* for at least fifteen minutes a day."

42. Kabbani, *Classical Islam and the Naqshbandi Sufi Tradition,* 172.

43. "Be aware of what catches your attention. Learn to withdraw your attention from undesirable objects. This is interpreted as: 'be vigilant in thought and remember yourself', *khawatir muraqaba."* Bennett. *The Masters of Wisdom,* 136.

44. Told to me by Michael Chokyi Dakpa Gregory in Boulder, Colorado, ca. 1999.

45. "Keeping out worldly thoughts by vigilant control of one's attention." Shushud, *Masters of Wisdom of Central Asia,* 33. Likewise, "the seeker must watch his heart and safeguard it by preventing bad thoughts from entering." Kabbani, *Classical Islam and the Naqshbandi Sufi Tradition,* 172.

46. *"[Yad]* (remembrance) is *[zikr]* and *kard* is the doing of the *[zikr]."* Kabbani, *Classical Islam and the Naqshbandi Sufi Tradition,* 170.

47. *Yad dasht* is "concentration upon the divine presence in a condition of *[zawq]."* Trimingham. *The Sufi Orders in Islam,* 203. "Be constantly aware of the Divine Presence. Become used to recognizing the Presence of God in your heart." Bennett, *Gurdjieff,* 35. "Recollection [...] in every breath without leaving the Presence of God." Kabbani, *Classical Islam and the Naqshbandi Sufi Tradition,* 173. *Yad dasht* is also "termed 'noting', this stands for becoming aware of Absolute Truth

as in some sense present." Shah, *A Perfumed Scorpion*, 86.

48. "Recollection *(yad dasht):* Constant awareness of the blissful presence of God [...] 'The complete experience of divine contemplation, achieved through the action of objective Love.'" Shushud, *Masters of Wisdom of Central Asia*, 33.

49. Kabbani, *Classical Islam and the Naqshbandi Sufi Tradition*, 173.

50. In the Naqshbandi lineage, they are expanded to eleven, adding three from Khwaja Baha' ad-Din Naqshband.

Chapter 5: The Three Deaths of Love

1. The outline of this story is found in the medieval Jewish mystical text *Reshit Hokhmah* by Eliyahu de Vidas, though it is almost certainly Sufi in origin. De Vidas writes there that one can see from this story how the love of a woman could bring us to the love of God. I first learned the story from my *murshid*, Zalman Schachter-Shalomi, of blessed memory (See Zalman Schachter. "The Source of Beauty." *The Message.* Vol. III, No. 8. August 1977: 0, 20, 24), who retold the story in English in a slightly longer form, and then from his wife, Eve Ilsen, a gifted storyteller who elaborated a still longer version. My own version, which has grown significantly over the years, is an elaboration of both.

2. *Fi Haqiqat al-'Ishaq*, translated as "On the Reality of Love" in Shihabuddin Yahya Suhrawardi. *The Philosophical Allegories and Mystical Treatises: A Parallel Persian-English Text.* Ed. & tr. Wheeler M. Thackston, Jr. Costa Mesa, CA: Mazda Publishers, 1999: 72.

3. Suhrawardi, *The Philosophical Allegories and Mystical Treatises*, 72.

4. Ibid., 72.

5. Two verses from the Song of Songs reversed, 8:7 and 8:6, as translated in Netanel Miles-Yépez (tr.). *My Love Stands Behind a Wall: A Translation of the Song of Songs and Other Poems: Second Expanded Edition.* Boulder, CO: Albion-Andalus Books, 2018: 41.

6. *Mesnavi*, Book V, 588-90. See William C. Chittick (ed. & tr.). *The Sufi Path of Love: The Spiritual Teachings of Rumi.* Albany, NY: State University of New York Press, 1983: 215.

7. Dick Davis (tr.). *Faces of Love: Hafez and the Poets of Shiraz.* Washington, DC: Mage Publishers, 2012: 48.

8. Ahmad Ghazzali actually speaks of a willingness to endure 'blame,' *malamat,* suggesting that this is a kind of ego-death, a death of self-interest. See Ahmad Ghazzali. *Sawanih: Inspirations from the World of Pure Spirits: The Oldest Persian Sufi Treatise on Love.* Tr. Nasrollah Pourjavady. Lahore, Pakistan: Suhail Academy, 1986: 23-27.

9. Ghazzali, *Sawanih,* 23, 25-26.

10. Anthony Mnghella (dir). *The English Patient.* Tiger Moth Productions, 1996. It is given here as in Mighella's screenplay. In Michael Ondaatje's novel, it is: "There are betrayals in war that are childlike compared with our human betrayals during peace. The new lovers enter the habits of the other. Things are smashed, revealed in a new light. This is done with nervous or tender sentences, although the heart is an organ of fire." Michael Ondaatje. *The English Patient.* Toronto: McClelland and Stewart, 1992.

11. My own telling is based on Gottfried von Strassburg, *Tristan, with the Surviving Fragments of the Tristan of Thomas.* Tr. A.T. Hatto. New York, NY: Penguin Books, 1960: 121-206. I have claimed a storyteller's privilege and retold it in my own way (though unconsciously), abridging certain elements and changing the order of events. It also reflects the influence and emphasis of Joseph Campbell's own tellings in: Joseph Campbell, with Bill Moyers. *The Power of Myth.* Ed. Betty Sue Flowers. New York, NY: Doubleday, 1988: 190; and Joseph Campbell. *Romance of the Grail: The Magic and Mystery of Arthurian Myth.* Ed. Evans Lansing Smith. Novato, CA: New World Library, 2015: 98-102.

12. In the "Alankaras" of the *Vadan* in Inayat Khan. *The Complete Sayings of Hazrat Inayat Khan.* New Lebanon, NY: Sufi Order Publications, 1978: 83. The love-potion is a "bowl of poison," as it "stands for something that threatens to overwhelm the senses and ultimately the will of the best-intentioned people, something that assails them from without, often suddenly, as a fate, something that infects their whole being to the point of frenzy—like a poison. 'Poison,' it must be said, is the form in which our Latin-derived word, 'potion' appears in Old French, and it means any draught that is drunk, whether for good or ill. In its baleful sense, 'poison' plays an important role in our story, since [Tristan] and [Isolde] not only drink the poison together, and with it their death [...]" A.T. Hatto's introduction to Gottfried von

Strassburg, *Tristan, with the Surviving Fragments of the Tristan of Thomas,* 7.

13. Ghazzali, *Sawanih,* 23, 26.

14. From the Anglican Christian wedding vows.

15. Ghazzali, *Sawanih,* 23, 26.

16. A saying of Rabi'a al-Basri repeated by Sufis in many forms.

17. *Divan-i Shams-i Tabrizi,* 65. See Chittick, *The Sufi Path of Love,* 242.

18. Inayat Khan. *The Bowl of Saqi: A Sufi Book of Days.* Ed. Netanel Miles-Yépez. Boulder, CO: Albion-Andalus Books, 2012: 11 (January 30).

19. Khan, *The Bowl of Saqi,* 13 (February 1), 65 (June 15), 91 (August 15).

20. *Mesnavi,* Book VI, 4304. Chittick, *The Sufi Path of Love,* 237.

21. As in the lyrics of the Daughter song: "If you're still bleeding, / you're the lucky ones, / 'cause most of our feelings, they are dead, and they are gone— / setting fire to our insides for fun, / collecting pictures from a flood that wrecked our home. / [. . .] And if you're in love, / then you are the lucky one, / 'cause most of us are bitter over someone— / setting fire to our insides for fun, / to distract our hearts from ever missing them." Daughter. "Youth." *If You Leave.* 4AD, 2013.

22. Updated and made gender-inclusive based on the "Alankaras" of the *Vadan* as found in Khan, *The Complete Sayings of Hazrat Inayat Khan,* 83-84.

Chapter 6: Meditation of the Heart

1. See Farid ad-Din 'Attar. *Farid ad-Din 'Attar's Memorial of God's Friends.* Tr. Paul Losensky. New York: Paulist Press, 2009: 374.

2. See 'Attar, *Farid ad-Din 'Attar's Memorial of God's Friends,* 105.

3. Netanel Miles-Yépez (ed.). *Meditations for InterSpiritual Practice: A Collection of Practices from the World's Spiritual Traditions: Second Edition.* Boulder, Colorado: Albion-Andalus Books, 2015: xx.

4. See chapter four of this book.

5. "Heaven and earth contain me not, but the heart of my faithful servant contains me." Javad Nurbakhsh. *Traditions of the Prophet: Volume 1.* New York: Khaniqahi-Nimatullahi Publications, 1981: 25 *Awarifu'l*

Ma'arif by Suhrawardi; *Ihya al-Olum* (Vol. 2, p. 250); *Ittehaf as-Sadat al-Mutaqin* (Vol. 7, p. 334).

6. See Javad Nurbakhsh. *The Path: Sufi Practices.* New York, NY: Khaniqahi Nimatullahi Publications, 2003: 162.

7. Kugle, *Sufi Meditation and Contemplation,* 78, and "You should know that contemplation *([muraqaba])* is a way for one to protect one's heart such that it cleaves to one single meaning and no other." Ibid., 76. "Then one closes one's eyes and, with the eyes of the heart, one gazes upon the heart and there one imagines that one is seeing God." Ibid., 85.

8. Inayat Khan. *Githas.* Githa 2: Ryazat 8. (Privately Circulated)

9. Khan, *Githas,* Githa 3: Dhyana 3. (Privately Circulated)

10. An extensive explanation of this practice can be found in Puran Bair and Susanna Bair. *Living from the Heart: Heart Rhythm Meditation for Energy, Clarity, Peace, Joy, and Inner Peace.* Tucson, AZ: Living Heart Media, 2009. The origin of the practice is described in the original edition of the book. Puran Bair. *Living from the Heart: Heart Rhythm Meditation for Energy, Clarity, Peace, Joy, and Inner Peace.* New York: Three Rivers Press, 1998: vii, 14-15.

11. The Eight Elements of Posture combine elements of the Seven Points of Vairochana in the Tibetan Buddhist tradition with Sufi instructions I received from Pir Puran Bair when I was initiated into the Heart Rhythm Meditation practice in June of 2002.

12. Bair, *Living from the Heart,* 100-03 (2009 Edition).

13. A number of traditional bases are discussed in Javad Nurbakhsh. *In the Paradise of the Sufis.* New York: Khaniqahi-Nimatullahi Publications, 1979: 79-80, not all encouraging a straight spine. Sufi meditation postures are also discussed in Inayat Khan. *Sangithas.* (Privately Circulated) What is important here, whatever posture taken, is to angle the thighs downward.

14. Creating a shape that reflects the Arabic word, *la,* or 'no.' Nurbakhsh, *In the Paradise of the Sufis,* 79.

15. Bair, *Living from the Heart,* 103 (2009 Edition).

16. Ibid.

17. Ibid.

18. Heard directly from Pir Puran Bair, his student.

19. Bair, *Living from the Heart,* 107-08 (2009 Edition).

20. Ibid., 107

21. Ibid. 127.

22. Ibid. 128.

23. Ibid. 129.

24. An insight capitalized on in Stanley Keleman's school of Formative Psychology.

25. Bair, *Living from the Heart,* 152 (2009 Edition).

26. Ibid., 134.

27. Ibid., 158.

28. "To perform this meditation, one should sit cross-legged. With the big toe of the right foot and its neighboring toe, compress the sciatic nerve behind the left knee. Then draw in the abdomen around the navel toward the back, from below until above." Kugle, *Sufi Meditation and Contemplation,* 64.

29. Bair, *Living from the Heart,* 155-57 (2009 Edition).

30. Edward W. Bastian and Tina L. Staley. *Living Fully, Dying Well: Reflecting on Death to Find Your Life's Meaning.* Ed. *Netanel Miles-Yépez.* Boulder, CO: Sounds True, 2009: 14-15.

31. Bastian, *Living Fully, Dying Well,* 15, 17.

32. Bair, *Living from the Heart,* 157-58 (2009 Edition).

33. Ibid.

34. Ibid., 158-59.

35. Ibid., 158.

36. Kugle, *Sufi Meditation and Contemplation,* 67. *Inayat Khan. Gathas.* Pasi Anfas. (Privately Circulated.)

37. Bair, *Living from the Heart,* 174-75, 190 (2009 Edition).

38. Described as a "Square Breath Rhythm" in Ibid., 188-96.

39. Khan, *Githas,* Githa 2: Ryazat 8. (Privately Circulated)

40. Kugle, *Sufi Meditation and Contemplation,* 92.

41. Bair, *Living from the Heart,* 174-75, 190 (2009 Edition).

42. Kugle, *Sufi Meditation and Contemplation,* 92.

43. Ibid., 91-92.

44. Here referring to the practice called *'Shaghal.'* Kugle, *Sufi Meditation and Contemplation,* 144. Referring to the same practice, Dara Shikuh says "This is called 'suspension of breath' *(habs-i nafas)*. Keep the breath suspended as long as you can easily do so without feeling suffocation." Ibid., 145 Elsewhere, "While suspending the breath, the mind should not remain idle because an idle mind gives opportunity for negative thoughts." Ibid., 146. And Shah Kalim Allah Jahanabadi, who says, "While reciting this with the heart, the breath must be suspended to such an extent that one repeats the above course two or three times with each breath. With practice, this can be extended to even more courses in each breath, up to 250 times! Doing this. generates internal heat that will burn away the greasy fat that congeals around the heart [...] Ibid., 64.

45. Called the "Square Breath" by Pir Puran Bair.

46. Bair, *Living from the Heart,* 188-89 (2009 Edition).

47. Transcription of an excerpt from "The Urs of Muinaddin Ajmiri," a talk by Pir Zia Inayat-Khan, ca. 2003.

Chapter 7: The Unity of All Being

1. See Muhyiddin ibn 'Arabi. *What the Seeker Needs: Essays on Spiritual Practice; The One Alone; Majesty and Beauty.* Trs. Tosun Bayrak and Rabia Harris. Putney, VT: Threshold Books, 1992: xii.

2. William Shakespeare. *Hamlet.* Act 2; Scene 2.

3. Ibn al-'Arabi. *The Bezels of Wisdom.* Tr. R.W.J. Austin. New York: Paulist Press, 1980: 146.

4. Most quotes in this chapter have been adapted from the originals for clarity and to be gender inclusive. See Ibn al-'Arabi, *The Bezels of Wisdom,* 283-84.

5. See Ibid., 282.

6. Ibid., 146.

7. See Ibid., 150-51.

8. Abraham Lincoln. "Meditation on Divine Will." Washington, D.C., September 2, 1862. A fragment written on a scrap of paper that was found and preserved by John Hay, one of President Lincoln's White House secretaries.

9. 'Gods of belief' is the basis of Hazrat Inayat Khan's 'God-ideal.'

10. A phrase used by philosopher, G.I. Gurdjieff.

11. Scott Kugle (ed.). *Sufi Meditation and Contemplation: Timeless Wisdom from Mughal India.* Tr. Scott Kugle and Carl Ernst. New Lebanon, NY: Suluk Press, 2012: 31.

12. Kugle, *Sufi Meditation and Contemplation,* 32.

13. An anecdote told by Sufis in various versions. For another classic version, see Farid ad-Din 'Attar. *Farid ad-Din 'Attar's Memorial of God's Friends.* Tr. Paul Losensky. New York: Paulist Press, 2009: 194-95.

14. In the Qur'an 6:22-24, it says God has no partners or associates, and Surah 31:13, says that associating anything with God is the worst sin.

15. Inayat Khan. *Sufi Prayers: The Prayers, Worship, and Remembrances of the Inayati Sufis.* Ed. Netanel Miles-Yépez. Boulder, CO: Albion-Andalus Books, 2015: 41.

16. See Ibn 'Arabi, *What the Seeker Needs,* 29.

17. See Ibid., 30, and Ibn 'Arabi. *"Whoso Knoweth Himself . . ."* Tr. T.H. Weir. London: Beshara Publications, 1976: 3.

18. Ibid., and Ibn 'Arabi, *"Whoso Knoweth Himself . . .,"* 3-4.

19. Ibid., and Ibn 'Arabi, *"Whoso Knoweth Himself . . .,"* 4.

20. Ibid., and Ibn 'Arabi, *"Whoso Knoweth Himself . . .,"* 4.

21. A translation of the famous Latin epigram found in the circa 12th century text, *Liber XXIV Philosophorum,* variously attributed to Aristotle or Hermes Trismegistus, *Deus est sphaera infinita, cuius centrum est ubique, circumferentia nusquam.* This is probably based on the earlier epigram, *Deus est sphaera intelligibilis cuius centrum ubique circumferential nusquam,* 'God is the intellectually knowable sphere whose center is everywhere and whose circumference is nowhere.' Alain de Lille, *Theologicae Regulae 7* (PL 210, 627), and quoted in Bonaventure, *Itinerarium mentis in Deum* V.8 (Quarrachi, ed., V.310). Later, Pascal substitutes "Nature" for "God."

22. See Ibn 'Arabi, *What the Seeker Needs,* 30, and Ibn 'Arabi, *"Whoso Knoweth Himself . . .,"* 4.

23. Ibid., xix.

24. Ibid., 32, and Ibn 'Arabi, *"Whoso Knoweth Himself . . .,"* 6-7.

25. William Shakespeare. *As You Like It.* Act II; Scene VII.

26. Khan, *Sufi Prayers* 41.

27. A treasured Sufi *ḥadith*, possibly based on the Qur'an, Surah 59:19: "Do not be like those who forgot *Allah*, who made them forget themselves."

28. See Ibn 'Arabi, *What the Seeker Needs*, 31, and Ibn 'Arabi, *"Whoso Knoweth Himself . . .,"* 4-5.

29. Told to me in East Lansing, Michigan, ca. 1997 or 1998, by John Allen Grimes, a philosopher of Advaita Vedanta, who was my mentor at Michigan State University.

30. See Ibn 'Arabi, *What the Seeker Needs*, 31, and Ibn 'Arabi, *"Whoso Knoweth Himself . . .,"* 5.

31. "Look, here is a tree in the garden, and every summer it produces apples, and we call it an 'apple tree,' because the tree *apples;* that's what it *does*. Alright, now here is a solar system inside a galaxy, and one of the peculiarities of this solar system is that—at least on the planet Earth—the thing *peoples*, in just the same way as an apple tree *apples*. … Because, you see, we grow out of this world in *exactly* the same way that the apples grow on the apple tree." Alan Watts. *The Tao of Philosophy 5: Myth of Myself.* 1965. (Recorded Talk).

32. A phrase used in Hasidism.

Chapter 8: The Stations of the Path

1. A.J. Arberry. *Sufism: An Account of the Mystics of Islam.* London: George Allen & Unwin Ltd., 1950: 75-79.

2. A good précis of them may be found in Arberry, *Sufism*, 75-79.

3. Inayat Khan. *Sufi Mysticism: The Sufi Message Series: Vol. 5.* "The Path of Initiation and Discipleship," Ch. 1.

4. Atum O'Kane (ed.). *The Leader's Manual: Volume 1: Leadership in the Sufi Order.* Seattle, WA: North American Secretariat of the Sufi Order, 1990: 289-90.

5. "It will be seen that al-Qushairi, despite the care with which he analyses the mystic's moral and psychological advance, did not always

mark carefully the distinction which later theorists observed between *maqam* and *hal.*" Arberry, *Sufism,* 79.

6. Robert Frager, *Heart, Self, & Soul: The Sufi Psychology of Growth, Balance, and Harmony.* Wheaton, IL: Quest Books, 1999: xi.

7. Retold based upon Frager, *Heart, Self, & Soul,* xvi-xxi.

8. "In order to earn God's pleasure the lover [Sufi] must carefully control his hand, his sex, and his tongue." Muzaffer Ozak. *The Unveiling of Love: Sufism and the Remembrance of God.* Tr. Muhtar Holland. New York: Pir Press, 2001: 161.

9. Yasar Nuri Öztürk. *The Eye of the Heart: An Introduction to Sufism and the Tariqats of Anatolia and the Balkans.* Tr. Richard Blakney. Istanbul: Redhouse Press, 1988: 28, 37.

10. Öztürk. *The Eye of the Heart,* 28, 37.

11. Ibid.

12. See Frager, *Heart, Self, & Soul,* xi-xii.

13. Heard from Michael Kosacoff in Boulder, Colorado, on Friday, July 29th, 2016, and on other occasions.

14. Carl W. Ernst and Bruce B. Lawrence. *Sufi Martyrs of Love: The Chishti Order in South Asia and Beyond.* New York: Palgrave Macmillan, 2002: 24-25. For examples of initiatory rites from other orders, see Javad Nurbakhsh. *In the Paradise of the Sufis.* New York: Khaniqahi-Nimatullahi Publications, 1979: 119-25, for Nimatullahi rites, and Shahab-u'd-din 'Umar b. Muḥammad Suhrawardi. *The 'Awarif-ul-Ma'arif.* Tr. H. Wilberforce Clarke. Lahore: Sh. Muhammad Ashraf, 1973: 286-291, for Qadiri rites.

15. "And We made the sky a canopy preserved . . ." Qur'an 21:32.

16. Ernst, *Sufi Martyrs of Love,* 24-25.

17. Heard from Michael Kosacoff in Boulder, Colorado, on Friday, July 29th, 2016, and on other occasions.

18. Yannis Toussulis and Mehmet Selim Baba, "Requisites of the Traveler *(Salik),*" *Eye of the Heart: A Newsletter of the Threshold Society.*

19. "Let the *salik* (pilgrim) ever be watchful during his journey, whatever the type of country through which he is passing, that he does not let his gaze be distracted from the goal of his journey. [...] The journey of the *salik,* though outwardly it is in the world, inwardly it is

with God." Spencer Trimingham. *The Sufi Orders in Islam.* New York, NY: Oxford University Press, 1971: 203.

20. See Javad Nurbakhsh. *In the Tavern of Ruin: Seven Essays on Sufism.* New York: Khaniqahi-Nimatullahi Publications, 1978: 76.

21. "Rumi often speaks of the relationship between teacher and student as that between the cook and the chickpea in the pot. 'You think I'm torturing you. I'm giving you flavor, so you can mix with rice and spices and be the lovely vitality of a human being.'" Coleman Barks, with John Moyne, A.J. Arberry, Reynold Nicholson (trs.). *The Essential Rumi.* Castle Books, Edison, NJ: 1995: 292.

22. Carl W. Ernst. *The Shambhala Guide to Sufism.* Boston: Shambhala Publications, 1997: 3.

23. "The third factor [to consider with regard to giving charity to others] is gratitude for benefits received, for the servant is indebted to God, Great and Gracious is He, for bounties both personal and material [..., for] there is no problem between the donor and the poor recipient until the former comes to regard himself as a benefactor." Al-Ghazali. *Inner Dimensions of Islamic Worship.* Tr. Muhtar Holland. Leicestershire, UK: The Islamic Foundation, 2012: 57, 63.

24. Toussulis, "Requisites of the Traveler *(Sālik).*"

25. "The Cherag conducts services, gives sermons, and performs all ceremonies of Universal Worship." *A Manual of Service for Universal Worship:* 3 (Privately Distributed)

26. Murat Yagan. *I Come from Behind Calf Mountain.* Putney, VT: Threshhold Books, 1984: 163.

27. When a certain name was mentioned as a possible successor, Khwaja Nizam ad-Din 'Awliyya responded, "The first requisite for this work is learning." Khaliq Ahmad Nizami. *The Life and Times of Shaikh Nizam-u'd-din Auliya.* Delhi: Idarah-i Adabyat-i Delhi: 1991: 158.

28. Nurbakhsh, *In the Tavern of Ruin,* 73.

29. Nizami, *The Life and Times of Shaikh Nizam-u'd-din Auliya,* 158.

30. Trimingham, *The Sufi Orders in Islam,* 173.

31. Gregory Blann. *Lifting the Boundaries: Muzaffer Efendi and the Transmission of Sufism to the West.* Nashville, TN: Four Worlds Publishing, 2005: 31.

32. Frager, *Heart, Self, & Soul,* xii.

33. Translated in Ernst, *Sufi Martyrs of Love,* 154. "Then he added, 'Four things are the jewels of the soul: helplessness which appears as power, hunger which appears as satiety, distress which appears as happiness, and friendship which appears even in the face of enmity. Every place that you go, keep your temper, and wherever you may be, act like a man.'" The four jewels of the soul, which Khwaja Mu'in ad-Din recommends may easily be misunderstood, but are important in terms of the *shaykh*'s authorization: vulnerability which is a strength, contentment while going without, finding happiness amid difficulties, and being friendly in the face of opposition. They are expectations and aspirations; it is expected that the *shaykh* aspire to these as a qualification for leadership.

34. Trimingham, *The Sufi Orders in Islam,* 192.

35. Based on admonitions in my own *ijazah,* which are taken from the *'Awarif al-Ma'arif* of Shahab ad-Din Suhrawardi. See Suhrawardi, *The 'Awarif-ul-Ma'arif,* 22-29.

36. Kelly Pemberton. "Women Pirs, Saintly Succession and Spiritual Guidance in South Asia." *The Muslim World.* Vol. 96. January 2006. 61-87.

37. Annmarie Schimmel. *Mystical Dimensions of Islam.* Chapel Hill, NC: University of North Carolina Press, 1975: 57.

38. "The *qutb* is the virtual center of spiritual energy upon whom the well-being of the world depends. [...] The *qutb* rests in perfect tranquility, grounded in God—that is why all the 'minor stars' revolve around him." Schimmel, *Mystical Dimensions of Islam,* 200.

39. Heard directly from Pir-o-Murshid Zalman Sulayman Schachter-Shalomi. According to Pir Zalman, Pir Vilayat also believed that Malkitzedek was the *qutb* in his time and passed the role to Abraham in the famous encounter described in Genesis. See also Blann. *Lifting the Boundaries,* 253: "Such a person often spiritually intercedes to help stop wars, mitigate disasters or bring succor to other souls." And Al-Hujwiri. *Revelation of the Mystery (Kashf al-Mahjub).* Tr. Reynold A. Nicholson. Accord, NY: Pir Press, 1999: 146-147, which says: "He was associated with the *[qutb]*, who is the pivot of the universe. On being asked to say who the *[qutb]* was, he did not declare his name but hinted that Junayd was the personage."

40. Al-Hujwiri, *Revelation of the Mystery (Kashf al-Mahjub)*, 228.

41. Ibid., 229. See Muhyiddin ibn 'Arabi. *What the Seeker Needs: Essays on Spiritual Practice; The One Alone; Majesty and Beauty.* Trs. Tosun Bayrak and Rabia Harris. Putney, VT: Threshold Books, 1992: xiii-xiv, for another account in which ibn 'Arabi meets the *qutb* in Egypt.

42. This notion is similar to that of the mystical tradition of Judaism which has thirty-six *tzaddikim nistarim* (hidden righteous), and a *tzaddik ha-dor* (righteous one of the generation).

43. See the story of the *qutb* in Frager, *Heart, Self, & Soul*, 16-17.

44. The theme of the *qutb* features prominently in two novels: Z'ev ben Shimon Halevi. *The Anointed: A Kabbalistic Novel.* Bet El Trust, 2013; and Ian Dallas. *The Book of Strangers.* Albany, NY: State University of New York Press, 1988.

Chapter 9: Sufism and the Inner Life

1. Heard from my first teacher of Sufism, Pir Vilayat's senior student, Thomas Atum O'Kane.

2. Inayat Khan. *Religious Gathekas*, #1. "If anybody asks you, 'What is Sufism?' . . . you may answer: 'Sufism is the religion of the heart, the religion in which the most important thing is to seek God in the heart of humanity.'"

3. While the 'message' is sometimes ambiguously discussed by Inayati Sufis, or generally equated with the teachings of Hazrat Inayat Khan, I believe it is simply the 'message of the unity of all being.'

4. "This is, of course, an extension into human history and cultural evolution of the biological principle that has helped in elucidating biological evolution: the principle that ontogeny, the history of the individual's developmental growth, is an epitome of phylogeny, the history of the race's development." Gerald Heard. *The Five Ages of Man: The Psychology of Human History.* New York: The Julian Press, 1963: 11.

5. An anecdote in the Hasidic oral tradition heard from Pir-o-Murshid Zalman Sulayman Schachter-Shalomi.

6. An anecdote in the Hasidic oral tradition heard from Pir-o-Murshid Zalman Sulayman Schachter-Shalomi.

7. *Bhagavad-Gita: The Song of God.* Trs. Swami Prabhavananda and Christopher Isherwood. Hollywood, CA: The Marcel Rodd Co., 1944: 121.

8. Inayat Khan. *The Art of Personality.* "Rasa Shastra." Chapter 3: Attraction and Repulsion.

9. Heard from Pir-o-Murshid Zalman Sulayman Schachter-Shalomi.

Glossary

abdāl (pl.) – Ara., Forty hidden saints placed around the world who support the work of the *qutb*, the fulcrum' of the generation.

'ahd – Ara., 'oath.'

ahl aṣ-ṣuffah – Ara., 'people of the bench.' The companions of the Prophet Muḥammad who sat outside the *masjid* in Medina.

aḥwāl (sing. *ḥāl*) – Ara., 'states.' Referring to temporary emotional states and states of consciousness.

akhdām (sing., *khādim*) – Ara., 'servitors.' Those who serve in the Sufi community.

'ālam-i wujūb – Ara./Per., 'world of will.'

alayhi as-salām (fem., *alayha as-salām*) – Ara., 'peace be upon him.'

Allāh – Ara., 'God.'

An al-Haqq – Ara., 'I am the Truth.'

ārifūn (sing., *'ārif*) – Ara., 'gnostics.'

ashab as-suffah – Ara., 'companions of the bench.' The companions of the Prophet Muḥammad who sat outside the *masjid* in Medina.

'ashaqah – Ara., A vine, like Bittersweet, which strangles a tree. Compared to the experience of being strangled by the intensity of a painful love, and considered the root of the word, *'ishq*.

'asmā' al-ḥusnā – Ara., 'beautiful names.' The ninety-nine 'beautiful names' of God found in the Qur'an.

bābā – Per., 'papa.' Among some Sufi orders, senior mentoring dervishes.

baraka – Ara., 'blessing.' Specifically, in the sense of spiritual power or transmission.

bay'ah – Ara., 'agreement,' 'covenant,' or 'deal.' Sufi initiation;

also called, 'taking hand.'

bay'at haqīqa – Ara., 'true agreement.' Formal initiation.

bāz – Ara., 'falcon.'

bāz gasht – Per., 'coming back' or 'returning.'

begum – Urd., A married woman of high rank.

bībī – Urd., 'lady.' A title of respect, generally meaning, 'lady.'

cāravānserāi – *Per.,* 'inn.'

chai – Per., 'tea.'

chaikhāna – Per., 'tea-house.'

chillā – Per., 'forty.' A forty-day of solitary retreat. In this context, the word came to have the connotation of 'ordeal.'

chillā'khāna – Per., 'place of forty' or 'ordeal.' Where the forty-day solitary retreat took place.

chirāgh (f. *chirāghah)* – Per., 'candle' or 'light.' A religious functionary of Universal Worship in most Inayati lineages, and a broader vocational role in the Inayati-Maimuni lineage.

dargāh – Per., 'burial shrine.' The burial place of a Sufi master; often a place of pilgrimage.

darvīsh (pl. *darāvīsh)* – Per., 'one who stands on the threshold.' A beggar. In the Sufi context, a beggar of God, or a mature Sufi. Also, dervish.

du'ā – Ara., 'extemporaneous prayer'

'eshq – Ara./Per., 'passionate love.'

'eshq-i haqīqī – Per., 'true love.' Love of God.

'eshq-i majāzī – Per., 'apparent love.' Human love.

fanā' – Ara., 'annihilation.' Annihilation or obscuration of the self. Better understood as making the self transparent to God.

fanā' fi-shaykh – Ara., 'annihilation in the *shaykh.'* Making one's self transparent to the *shaykh.*

faqīr (f. *faqīrah*) – Ara., 'one who is poor.' A beggar. In the Sufi context, a beggar of God, or a mature Sufi.

fikr – Ara., 'contemplation.' The Sufi practice of contemplation, or of placing a *wazīfa* on the breath.

firāq – 'separation.'

fuqarā' (sing., *faqīr*) – Ara., 'poor ones.' A Sufi circle or community.

ghauth – Ara., 'help.' The focal point of God's supervision on Earth. Another term for *qutb.*

habs-i nafas – Per., 'suspension of breath.'

ḥadīth – Ara., 'report' or 'tradition.' A report of words or deeds of the prophet Muḥammad in the Islamic tradition.

hadīth qudsī – Ara., 'holy report' or 'tradition.' A non-Qur'anic report of the words of God uttered by the prophet Muḥammad, but remembered in the Islamic tradition.

halqah – Ara., 'ring' or 'circle.' A circle, small group, or community of Sufis.

al-Haqq – Ara., 'the Truth' or 'the Reality.' God.

hōsh dar dam – Ara., 'mind on the breath.'

hubb – Ara., 'love.'

hukamā (sing., *hakīm*) – Ara., 'wise ones.' An early name for Sufis.

huzūr – Ara., 'presence.' God's presence.

'ibādah – Ara., 'worship.'

ijāzah-nāma – Ara., 'letter of authorization.' Document signifying succession as a Sufi master.

Ilāhī-anta maqsudī wa-ridhaka matlubī – Ara., 'My God, you are my goal, and your pleasure my desire.'

'inshā-Allāh – Ara., 'God willing.'

'iqrār – Ara., 'pledge' or 'promise.' One wishing to be admitted to the initiation rites of the Sufis.

irshād – Ara., 'guidance.' Spiritual guidance.

'ishq (alt. *'eshq*) – Ara., 'passionate love.'

'Ishq Allāh, ma'būd Allāh – Ara., 'God love, God beloved.'

itlāq – Ara., 'liberation.'

jahannam – Ara.,'hell.'

janna – Ara., 'paradise.'

ka'bah – Ara.,'cube.' The 'axis mundi' and central shrine of Islam in Mecca.

kalimah – Ara.,'word.' The phrase *Lā 'ilāha 'illā llāh.* See *shahāda* and *tahlīl.*

kalimat-i qudsiyya – Per., 'sacred words.' The eight principles of the Khwajaghan.

kashkūl – Per., 'begging bowl.'

khādim (pl., *akhdām*) – Ara., 'servitor.' A servant in the Sufi community.

khalīfa (pl., *khulafā'*) – Ara., 'deputy' or 'steward.' A successor and representative of a *shaykh* or *murshid.*

khalwah – Ara., 'seclusion' or 'isolation.' Sufi retreat.

khalwah bātinah – Ara., 'internal solitude.'

khalwah zāhirah – Ara., 'external solitude.'

khānegāh – Per., 'place' or 'traveler's house.' A building used for Sufi gatherings and dedicated to Sufi life and practice. The same as a *zāwiyah, ribat,* or *tekke.*

khayālāt – 'dream state.'

khilāfat-nāma – Ara., 'letter of succession.' Document signifying succession as a Sufi master.

khilvat dar anjuman – Ara., 'solitude in the crowd.'

khirqa – Ara., 'rag' or 'cloak.' A Sufi cloak.

khwāja – Per., 'master of wisdom.'

khwājaghān – Per., 'masters of wisdom.'

Lā 'ilāha 'illā llāh hū – Ara., 'There is no God; nevertheless, God is.'

mahabba – Ara., 'love.' Love in general, or baseline love.

malak – Ara., 'messenger' or 'angel.'

maqām (pl., *maqāmāt*) – Ara., 'place' or 'station.' A level of sustained integration achieved by a Sufi, and sometimes marked by a specific role or responsibility in the Sufi community.

ma'rifah – Ara., 'gnosis' or 'experiential knowledge.'

masjid – Ara., 'place of prostration' or 'mosque.'

mawlā – Ara., 'master.'

mazhab-i 'eshq – Per., 'school of love.'

muḥāsaba – Ara., 'reckoning' or 'accounting.' The Sufi practice of reflecting on one's actions.

muhibb (f. *muhibba*) – Ara., 'one who loves.' An admirer of Sufism or a Sufi community.

muḥtarima – 'lady.' A title of respect, generally meaning, 'lady.'

murāqaba – Ara., 'to watch over.' Meditation, or the Sufi meditative technique of absorbing the mind.

murāqaba al-qalb – Ara., 'meditation of the heart.'

murīd (f. *murīda,* pl., *murīdun*) – Ara., 'seeker.' An initiate in a Sufi lineage.

murshid (f. *murshida*) – Ara., 'guide.' The leader of a Sufi community. Parallel to *shaykh,* and sometimes *pir.*

mūtū qabla an tamūtū – Ara., 'die before death.'

nafas bātin – Ara., 'subtle breath.'

nafs – Ara., 'ego, 'self,' 'soul,' or 'essence.'

nafs al-ammāra – Ara., 'tyrannical self.'

nafs al-lawwama – Ara., 'regretful self.'

nawāfil – Ara., 'supererogatory practice.' Practicing beyond the norm.

nazar bar qadam – Ara., 'watch your step.'

nigāh dāsht – Per., 'watchfulness' or 'attentiveness.'

nussāk (sing. *nāsik*) – Ara., 'ascetics.'

pas-i anfas – *Per.,* 'observing the breaths.'

pir – Per., 'elder.' The leader of a Sufi community, parallel to *shaykh* and *murshid.* In Inayati Sufism the head of an Inayati lineage (formal title, *pir-o-murshid*).

pirāni – Per., 'wife of the *pir.*'

pirī-murīdī – Per., '*pir-murīd.*' The relationship between Sufi master and disciple.

pir-mā – Per., 'mother of the *pir.*'

pir-o-murshid (f. *pirnī/pirain-o-murshida*) – Per./Ara., 'elder and guide.' In Inayati Sufism the head of an Inayati lineage.

qabilah – Ara., 'tribe.'

qasab – Ara., 'tubes.' A Chishti Sufi practice.

qawwāli – Urd., '[comprised] of utterances.' The Sufi musical form of the Chishti *tarīqah.* The word is based on *qaul,* an 'utterance' of the prophet.

qurb – Ara., 'proximity.'

qutb – Ara., 'axis' or 'pole.' The fulcrum of humanity in any given age.

rābita – Ara., 'bond.' The internal bond between a Sufi initiate and their master.

safā – Ara., 'pure.'

safar dar vatan – Ara., 'journey homeward' or 'journey in your homeland.'

sāhiba – 'lady.' A title of respect, generally meaning, 'lady.'

sajjāda-nishīn – 'one who sits on the carpet.' A Sufi master or leader.

salāh – Ara., 'Islamic prayer.'

sālik (f. *sālika,* pl., *sālikun*) – Ara., 'traveler.' One who walks the spiritual path, or a competent Sufi.

samā – Ara., 'hearing.' Practice of courting ecstasy with music and dance and the recitation of love poetry.

shafa' – Ara., 'healing.'

shafa'a – Ara., 'interceding.'

shahāda – 'testimony.' The phrase *Lā 'ilāha 'illā llāh.* See *kalimah* and *tahlīl.*

shajara sharīf – Ara., 'noble tree.' The graphic depiction of a Sufi *silsila.*

shathiyāt (sing. *shath*) – Ara., 'ecstatic utterance.'

shawq – Ara., 'yearning.'

shaykh (f. *shaykha*, pl., *shuyūkh*) – Ara., 'elder.' The leader of a Sufi community, parallel to *pir* and *murshid.*

shaykh as-sajjāda – Ara., 'elder of the carpet.' A Sufi master or leader.

shirk – Ara., 'association.' The heresy of associating partners with God.

silsila – Ara., 'chain.' The line of succession or the chain of transmission of a lineage.

soḥbet (Ara., *suḥbah*) – Tur., 'fellowship' or 'companionship.' The context and activity of Sufi teaching and fellowship.

sūf – Ara., 'wool.'

ṣuffah – Ara., 'bench.'

sūfiyya – Ara., 'wool wearers.' Sufis.

sulūk – Ara., 'journey.'

sūq – Ara., 'market.'

tafakkur – Ara., 'deep contemplation.'

tahlīl – Ara., 'praise.' The phrase *Lā 'ilāha 'illā llāh.* See *kalimah* and *shahāda.*

tālib (f. *tāliba,* pl., *tālibun*) – Ara., 'candidate.' A candidate for entry into the Sufi path.

tanbīh – Ara., 'awakening' or 'reproof.'

tarīqah (pl., *turuq*) – Ara., 'path' or 'order.' The Sufi path, or a particular Sufi lineage.

tasawwuf – Ara., 'purification.' Sufism.

tasawwur-i murshid – Per., 'visualization of the guide.'

tesbīḥ – Ara., 'tool of glorification' or 'glorifier.' A string of ninety-nine beads used to keep count during *zikr*.

tawakkul – Ara., 'trust' or 'reliance.' Trust in or reliance on God.

tawba – Ara., 'turning' or 'turning back.' Turning back to God, repentance, or conversion.

tawḥīd – Ara., 'unity.' The teaching of God's radical oneness.

tekke – Tur., 'refuge.' A building used for Sufi gatherings and dedicated to Sufi life and practice. The same as a *zāwiyah, ribat,* or *khānegāh*.

uns – Ara., 'intimacy.'

usrah – Ara., 'family.'

waḥdat al-wujūd – Ara., 'unity of all being' or 'existence.' The radical teaching of non-duality in Sufism. In Inayati Sufism, expressed by the phrase, 'the message.'

wajd – Ara., 'ecstasy.'

wazīfa (pl., *wazā'if*) – Ara. Mantra, sacred word or formula.

wusūl – Ara., 'union.'

yād dāsht – Per., 'remembrance.'

yād kard – Per., 'remembering.' Equivalent to the Arabic, *zikr*.

Ya Rahīm – Ara., 'O most merciful.'

Ya Rahmān – Ara., 'O most compassionate.'

zākir – Ara., 'remember-er.' A leader or practitioner of *zikr*.

zawq (*dhawq*) – Ara., 'taste' or 'tasting.' Immediate experience.

zikr (*dhikr*) – Ara., 'remembrance.' The practice of remembering God through repetition of a divine name or sacred formula.

zikr Allāh – Ara., 'remembrance of God.'

zikr jahrī – Ara., 'vocal remembrance.'

zikr khafī – Ara., 'silent remembrance.'

zira'a – Ara., 'cultivation.'

Index

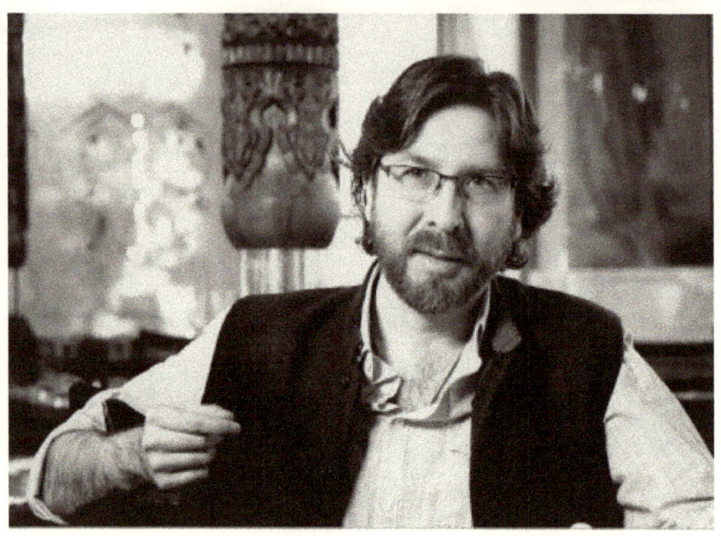

Pir Netanel (Mu'in ad-Din) Miles-Yépez is the current head of the Inayati-Maimuni Order of Sufism.

An artist, writer, philosopher, and scholar of comparative religion, Pir Netanel first studied History of Religions at Michigan State University and then Contemplative Religion at the Naropa Institute before pursuing traditional studies and training in both Sufism and Hasidism with his *pir* and *rebbe*, Zalman Schachter-Shalomi, the famous pioneer in interfaith dialogue and comparative mysticism.

Pir Netanel is the translator of *My Love Stands Behind a Wall: A Translation of the Song of Songs and Other Poems* (2015), co-author of two critically acclaimed commentaries on Hasidic spirituality, *A Heart Afire: Stories and Teachings of the Early Hasidic Masters* (2009) and *A Hidden Light: Stories and Teachings of Early HaBaD and Bratzlav Hasidism* (2011), and the editor of various works on Sufism and InterSpirituality.

Currently, Pir Netanel lives in Boulder, Colorado, where he is a professor in the Department of Religious Studies at Naropa University, and from which he leads the Inayati-Maimuni Order.

www.ingramcontent.com/pod-product-compliance
Lightning Source LLC
Chambersburg PA
CBHW020152090426
42734CB00008B/794

* 9 7 8 1 7 3 4 8 7 5 0 9 6 *